THE PERSIAN ṢŪFIS

CYPRIAN RICE, O.P.

London

GEORGE ALLEN & UNWIN LTD

RUSKIN HOUSE MUSEUM STREET

First published in 1964

PRINTED IN GREAT BRITAIN
in 10 *on* 11 *point Old Style type*
BY C. TINLING AND CO. LTD
LIVERPOOL, LONDON AND PRESCOT

ONE

INTRODUCTORY

THE Ṣūfi phenomenon is not easy to sum up or define. The Ṣūfis never set out to found a new religion, a *mazhab* or denomination. They were content to live and work within the framework of the Moslem religion, using texts from the Qorān much as Christian mystics have used the Bible to illustrate their tenets. Their aim was to purify and spiritualize Islām from within, to give it a deeper, mystical interpretation, and infuse into it a spirit of love and liberty. In the broader sense, therefore, in which the word religion is used in our time, their movement could well be called a religious one, one which did not aim at tying men down with a new set of rules but rather at setting them free from external rules and open to the movement of the spirit.

This religion was disseminated mainly by poetry, it breathed in an atmosphere of poetry and song. In it the place of great dogmatic treatises is taken by mystical romances, such as Yusuf and Zuleikha or Leila and Majnūn. Its one dogma, an interpretation of the Moslem witness: 'There is no god but God', is that the human heart must turn always, unreservedly, to the one, divine Beloved.

Who was the first Ṣūfi? Who started this astonishing flowering of spiritual love in lyrical poetry and dedicated lives? No one knows.

Early in the history of Islām, Moslem ascetics appeared who, from their habit of wearing coarse garments of wool (*ṣúf*), became known as Ṣūfis. But what we now know as Ṣūfism dawned unheralded, mysteriously, in the ninth century of our era and already in the tenth and eleventh had reached maturity. Among all its exponents there is no single one who could be claimed as the initiator or founder.

Ṣūfism is like that great oak-tree, standing in the middle of the meadow: no one witnessed its planting, no one beheld its beginning, but now the flourishing tree speaks for itself, is true to origins which it has forgotten, has taken for granted.

There is a Ṣūfi way, a Ṣūfi doctrine, a form of spiritual knowledge known as *'irfán* or *ma'rifat,* Arabic words which correspond to the Greek gnosis.

Ṣūfism has its great names, its poet-preachers, its 'saints', in the broad, irenical sense in which the word can be used. Names like Maulānā Rumi, Ibn al 'Arabi, Jámi, Mansúr al Halláj are household words in the whole Islamic world and even beyond it.

Has it a future? Perhaps we may say that if, in the past, its function was to spiritualize Islám, its purpose in the future will be rather to make possible a welding of religious thought between East and West, a vital, oecumenical commingling and understanding, which will prove ultimately to be, in the truest sense, on both sides, a return to origins, to the original unity.

When one speaks of the Ṣūfis as 'mystics', one does not necessarily mean to approve all their teaching or all their methods, nor, indeed, admit the genuineness of the mystical experiences of this or that individual. But whatever one's preconceptions or reservations, it is difficult, after a careful study of their lives and writings, not to recognize a kinship between the Ṣūfi spirit and vocabulary and those of the Christian saints and mystics.

This book is concerned mainly with the Persian mystics. Taken all in all, what goes by the name of 'Islāmic mysticism' is a Persian product. The mystical fire, as it spread rapidly over the broad world of Islām, found tinder in the hearts of many who were not Persians: Egyptians like Dhu'l Nun, Andalucians like Ibn'ul Arabi, Arabs like Rabi'a al 'Adawiyya. But Persia itself is the homeland of mysticism in Islám. It is true that many Islamic mystical writers, whether Persian or not, wrote in Arabic, but this was because that language was in common use throughout the Moslem world for the exposition of religious and philosophical teaching. It could, indeed, be said that the Persians themselves took up the Arabic language and forged from it the magnificent instrument of precise philosophical and scientific expression which it became, after having been used by the Arabs themselves almost exclusively for poetry. This was Persia's revenge for the humiliating defeat she suffered at the hands of the Arabs and the consequent imposition of the Arabic language for all religious and juridical purposes. We might go on to say that Persia's revenge for the imposition of Islām and of the Arabic Qorān was her bid for the utter transformation of the religious outlook of all the Islamic peoples by the dissemination of the Ṣūfi creed and the creation of a body of mystical poetry which is almost as widely known as the Qorān itself. The combination in Ṣūfism of mystical love and passion with a daring challenge to all forms of rigid and hypocritical formalism has had a bewitching and breath-taking effect on successive Moslem generations in all countries, an effect repeated in all those non-Moslem milieux, European or Asiatic, where these doctrines, often interpreted by the most ravishingly beautiful poetry, have been discovered. In this way Persia has conquered a spiritual domain far more extensive than any won by the arms of Cyrus and Darius, and one which is still far from being a thing of the past. Indeed, one might say that through this mystical lore, expressed in an incomparable poetical medium, Persia found herself, discovered something like her true spiritual vocation among the peoples of the world, and that her voice has now only to make itself heard to win the delighted approval of all those seekers and connoisseurs whose souls are attuned to perceive the message of the *ustād i azāl* (the eternal master), to use Khojá Ḥáfiẓ's phrase.

In a sense, this bold transformation of Islām from within by the mystical mind of Persia began already in the Prophet's life-time with the part played in the elaboration and interpretation of Mahomet's message by the strange but historic figure of Salmān Fārsi—Salmān the Persian—to whom M. Massignon devoted an indispensable monograph. But a similar influence revealed itself in the rapid spiritualization of the person of 'Ali and the parallel evolution of the mystical significance of Mahomet, around the notion of the *nūr muḥammadi*—the

'Mahomet-light', which seems to amount to the introduction of a Logos doctrine into the heart of Islām, viewed as an esoteric system. The influences, as they worked themselves out, led, on the other hand, to the formation of the Shi'a, involving the spiritual-mystical significance accorded to the Imám. At the same time, the teaching and outlook of Mahomet himself was progressively brought into conformity with the Ṣūfi model by the accumulation of a large body of *aḥādith* (traditional sayings) fathered onto the Prophet by successive generations.

The vigour of the Persian spiritual genius, however, is not a phenomenon which came suddenly to light at the outset of Islám. It was there all the time, and there are Persians whom I have known who claim that the stream of pure Persian mysticism has pursued its course, now open, now hidden, right down the ages. This is a claim which springs, maybe, more from the Persians' own intuition than from any positive documentation, but the assumption comes out clearly in the writings of Suhravardi and the Ishráqi school. In any case, one cannot but be struck by the atttraction exerted and the penetration achieved by Persian religions, such as Mithraism and Manichaeism, as far afield as the farthest frontiers of the Roman Empire, as well as in farthest Asia and who knows where else. The Christian Church of Persia itself, which, as Mgr Duchesne has pointed out, rivalled even the Church of Rome in the number of its martyrs, sent its missionaries far and wide throughout Asia, into India, China and Japan. As to the exploits of Christian missionaries from Persia in Japan, facts are only now coming to light through the investigations of Prof. Sakae Ikeda. Japanese writers have also traced deep influences of Persian Christianity in the emergence of the Mahayána type of Buddhism in China.

If these facts are recorded here, it is merely in order to make it clear that the universal radiation of the Persian spirit was not confined to the Islamic world.

Words like *ma'rifat* or *irfán* used to designate Ṣūfi teaching might lead one to conclude that theirs was essentially a speculative movement. But one must always bear in mind that it is fundamentally a practical science, the teaching of a way of life. This aspect of it was most clearly marked, no doubt, in its earlier period but it has remained as a permanent feature of the Ṣūfi system and all its professors are agreed that those who enter on the search for perfection must needs undergo a rigorous course of training under a wise spiritual father (*Pir u Murshid*). In a great mystical writer like Jalál-edDin Rúmi, for instance, the most sublime mystical descriptions are never entirely divorced from moral exhortations. It is true that for Rúmi the moral virtues are never ends in themselves. They are seen as ways and means, creating the necessary conditions for the attainment of closer union with the divine Beloved. But that does but make his exhortations more pressing.

Some readers may question the use of the term 'mystical' in this field, or may ask for it to be defined. In brief the reply shall be that the term is used here to signify doctrines concerning the way to God or to perfection derived from inner experience and inspiration rather than from deductive reasoning or positive tradition. Something of what is meant can be found in Sheikh 'Aṭṭār's words, in his introduction to the *Memoirs of the Saints*. He recommends the study of the sayings of the great mystics because, as he says, 'their utterances are the result of spiritual enterprise and experience, not of mechanical learning and repetition of what others have said. They spring from direct insight and not from discursive reasoning, from supernatural sources of knowledge, not from laborious personal acquisition. They gush forth as from the source and are not painfully conveyed over man-made aqueducts. They come from the sphere of "My Lord has educated me" and not from the sphere of "my father told me".'

The lesser lights among Ṣūfi poets have only too often repeated the images and allegories used by their greater predecessors, making of them mere clichés, hackneyed and hollow. Indeed, the bane of Persian mystical poetry is the incalculable number of its mediocre practitioners.

Leaving them aside, we do well to concentrate on the great masters, such as, among poets, Jalál-edDin Rúmi, Farid edDin 'Aṭṭār, Maghribi, Jámi, Hāfiz, and among prose-writers, Hujviri, al-Sarráj, Najm-edDin Rázi, and, once again, 'Aṭṭār, with his indispensable *Memoirs of the Saints*. Nor should one exclude from any enumeration of Persian mystics the name of Mansúr al-Halláj, a native of Fárs, in the heart of old Irán, even though he wrote in Arabic (and with what clarity, simplicity and force!). Without attempting a complete enumeration, one cannot refrain from mentioning names like Hakim Sanái, Shabistari, author of the *Gulshan i Ráz*, and Abu Said of Mihneh.

For many centuries this abundant store of mystical wisdom was a closed book for the West. The medieval schoolmen came to know Persian philosophers such as Avicenna (Ibn Siná) and el Gazel (Ghazáli) through Hebrew and Latin translations but there is no trace of their having suspected the existence of Persian mystical writings. It is possible, however, that an indirect influence was exercised by Moslem mystical poems on the Troubadours.

In this country, it was not until 1774 that Sir William Jones' Latin *Commentaries on Asiatic Poetry* opened the way to knowledge of the Persian writers but the work, inevitably perhaps, created little stir and bore scarcely any fruit.

It was in Germany, in the Romantic period, that the great *éblouissement* came. Goethe's *West-östlicher Diwan* was the first consequence of it. Ruckert, Herder and others set themselves with great zeal and application to study Persian mystical verse and to make it the leaven of the new poetical and philosophical movement in their country.

During the present century German interest in Persian mysticism was revived by Kāẓimzādeh Irānshahr, a Persian who settled in Berlin and published a number of religious booklets based upon Ṣūfi teachings.

Meanwhile, in England the study of Persian literature was immensely forwarded by the masterly and abundant work of Professor E. G. Browne of Cambridge. Browne, moreover, had the good fortune to find in R. A. Nicholson, later to be his successor in the Chair of Arabic at Cambridge, a scholar in whom the study of Persian poetry kindled and fed an inborn affinity with mystical learning. The result was his annotated edition of a selection of mystical odes from the *Diván of Shams of Tabriz*, by Jalālu' ddin Rūmi, in 1898.

Later on, Nicholson contributed to the Gibb Series his edition of Hujviri's *Kashful Maḥjūb* and then Sarrāj's *Kitābul Luma'*, both of which are key works for the study of Ṣūfi doctrine.

Then came his magnum opus, the great new edition of the text of Rúmi's *Mathnaviyi Ma'navi*, the 'bible of the Ṣūfis', followed, within the next fifteen years, by a translation of the whole work and finally by a full commentary, in which Professor Nicholson revealed the full extent of his mastery of the subject.

He had, moreover, in 1905, laid students still further under an obligation to him by his critical edition, in two volumes, of Sheikh 'Attār's invaluable *Taẕkirat ul Awliya*, a collection of biographies of a number of well-known and less-known Ṣūfis and saints of the Moslem world.

For the general public, Professor Nicholson wrote a valuable little book in the 'Quest' series, called *The Mystics of Islam*, as well as *Studies in Islamic Mysticism* and *The Idea of Personality in Ṣūfism*—in addition to numerous articles in encyclopaedias and journals, the ransom of his unique reputation: for there is no doubt that, as *The Times* wrote in the obituary notice published after his death, on August 27, 1945, 'Nicholson was the greatest authority on Islamic mysticism this country has produced, and in his own considerable field the supreme authority in the world'.

In any final assessment, however, it would be difficult to give the late Professor Louis Massignon, chiefly noted for his exposition of the mystic teaching of al-Ḥallāj, any lower place. Both of them were so deeply penetrated by the Ṣūfi spirit that they would have shrunk with horror from any such competition.

Professor A. J. Arberry, Nicholson's successor in the Chair of Arabic at Cambridge, has also rendered valuable services to the study of Islamic mysticism by his edition of Kalabādhi's treatise on Ṣūfism, as well as by other books intended to make Persian mystics known to a wide public. In 1950 he contributed to the series of 'Ethical and Religious Classics of East and West' an account of the mystics of Islam, called *Ṣūfism*.[1] It can

[1] Published by George Allen and Unwin, Ltd.

be recommended as a clear, orderly and sympathetic account of the subject which aims at leaving out none of the facts, writings and personalities that count in a serious study of Islamic mysticism.

Thus helped and stimulated, we have now to take up the legacy bequeathed to us and ensure that these works shall be pored over as studiously as they deserve, their lessons learnt and their indications followed up. A legacy of this kind is, at the same time, a challenge, above all to those whose task or vocation it is to bring about a reconciliation of East and West, or to prepare the ground for religious agreement on a plane which transcends the bare statement of controversial issues, led rather by the spirit of Juan de Segovia, whose motto was *Per viam pacis et doctrinae.*

Perhaps, too, the study of these mystics, who had to find their way through pathless deserts without the sure guidance of an unerring authority, and who, nevertheless, reached in the main a surprisingly convincing statement of mystical truth, may have the further advantage of giving us pause and of inspiring us with humility, when we realize what mystical treasures we ourselves may have let slip through carelessness or dissipation.

If, in this study, I have, in the main, used the language of Christian mysticism this is partly because it has now become the custom of Western writers—not least among whom we must count Don Miguel Asin Palacios—to do so. Then I consider this custom justified by reason of the similar workings of God with souls in every climate and the similar response human souls make to Him whatever be their form of speech.

At the same time, needless to say, I would not wish it to be thought that I am therefore claiming that Billuart or Bossuet necessarily attached the same meaning to the terms here used as would Rúmi or Bistámi. It is just a matter of human interpretation, aiming at broad parallels rather than at precise identification. Don Palacios has spoken of certain Ṣūfi teachings as *un Islám cristianizado*. By doing so he clearly shows that, in his opinion, the similarities just referred to go deeper than forms of language as such. Of Ibn Abbád of Ronda Don

Palacios says that here is 'a hispano Moslem precursor of St John of the Cross'. He finds in him 'a profoundly Christian attitude of abandonment to the charismatic gifts (*karimát*)'.

Perhaps I may be allowed to add that in taking this line with the Ṣūfi mystics I conform to the wish expressed so ardently by the late Pope John XXIII, in an address to a general meeting of Benedictine Abbots in Rome. Setting before them the ideal of the union of souls, he exhorted them to consider, 'not so much what divided minds as what brings them together'.

As this modest volume is to appear at the time of an Oecumenical Council in which relations between the Church of East and West are expected to form one of the dominant themes, the writer ventures to express the hope that a study of some of the aspects of Islamic mysticism may contribute to a better understanding of the inner life of the vast Mahometan populations of Asia and Africa. Under the ample umbrella of Islam, with its one compendious dogma *Lā ilāha illá 'llāh*—'There is no god but God'—a vast assortment of religious doctrines and devotional practices shelter. Much of this originated in regions of western Asia where Christianity had reached a notable expansion and where Christian monasticism made a strong appeal to the religious sentiments of the various peoples who, sooner or later, yielded to political or military pressure and ranged themselves, willingly or unwillingly under the banner of Mahomet. The mystical teachings of the early centuries were diffused throughout western Asia, not least in Syria and Persia. There can be little doubt that much of that teaching was passed on to subsequent generations after the Moslem conquest. The devout, in their insatiable hunger for religious truth and experience, not only took up the mystical teaching they found but in many ways made it their own, re-thought it and developed it in original ways.

In the *Divine Comedy* (Inferno, Canto 28) Dante pictures Mahomet and 'Ali among the authors of schism, alongside a varied band of Italians. Such a view of the role of Mahomet has its bearing on our theme. In any effort to bring about an understanding between East and West, it would be unrealistic, to say the least, to leave out of account the numerous Mahometan populations among whom Eastern Christians live and move.

In all fairness, too, one must add that Mahomet's dream was not to foster, but rather to heal the schism between minds, as he looked out upon the disputes of the numerous Christian sects and rites on Arabian and near-Arabian soil. It would seem that he dreamt of reconciling all by proposing adhesion to a single dogma on which all could agree: 'There is no god but God'. It was of this proclamation or 'gospel' that he was the Prophet.

TWO

THE ṢŪFI MOVEMENT

THOSE then who, in Persia and elsewhere in the world of Islam, devoted themselves to the practice and dissemination of ascetical and mystical doctrine soon became known as 'Ṣūfis', a name given them because, as we saw, they chose to wear a distinguishing dress of coarse, undyed wool (*ṣūf*), a type of dress already worn by Christian ascetes in the East. Later on, this habit was in general replaced by the *khirqa*, or patched frock, which was given by the Pir or sheikh to the novice whom he accepted as his disciple (*murid*).

This Ṣūfi movement was not itself an order or a sect. Many confraternities, based on Ṣūfi principles and ideals, did arise in course of time and, in a number of cases, still survive, although the times are against them. Lacking adequate religious control, these *tariqas*, as they are called, have, in many cases, lost much of their original fervour and distinction. They were suppressed by Kemál Ataturk in Turkey and in Persia Rizá Khán followed suit. In Cairo they are still numerous and active. Beloved by the common people, they are looked down upon by the better educated classes. It is to be hoped that, when the rage for Western journalism and films has passed, the modern generation in Persia will return to the treasures of the past and find in them a valid message for our age.

In the early years of the Moslem conquests, the Ṣūfis constituted a powerful reaction against worldliness and hypocrisy. Their reaction took the form, not so much of sermonizing, as of the example they gave of a life of self-denial, compunction, silence, poverty and detachment.

The leaders of this ascetic campaign were drawn at first chiefly from among the Arabs. But, as time went on and the reins of power passed more and more into Persian hands after the setting up of the Abbasid Caliphate in A.D. 750, the Iranian genius for interiorization and abstraction began to prevail over the more external preferences of the Semites.

It was seen that the true cause of repentance lay in the overriding urgency of loving God above all things, that human works, however good and virtuous, needed to yield pride of place to divine, prevenient grace, that the external (*ẓāhir*) must yield to the interior (*bāṭin*), the matter to the meaning, the outward symbol to the inner reality, cold reason to inspired and fiery love, self to the one Beloved. There were no limits to this way, once it had been entered upon. And it *was* entered upon, and run, with immense and reckless enthusiasm, even though it led at times to seeming antinomianism and unbelief (*kufr*). All this in the name of and for the glory of the central dogma of Islam, the unity of God, that *tawḥid* which came, for the Ṣūfi, to signify a mystico monistic outlook on the universe. A hard-headed, matter of fact Westerner is often put off or irritated by the wilfully extravagant *shathiyyāt* (jubilations, exclamations) of bold spirits such as al Hallāj or Bāyazid Bisṭāmi, when they cry: *Anā'l Ḥaqq* (I am God) or *Subḥāni* (Glory be to Me alone!). Such things, however, are explained to us as having their origin in the fact that these men had been led to transcend their own personalities and to become conscious only of HIM (the pronoun commonly used by such mystics in referring to God, considered as having, in the last resort, the exclusive right to declare I AM). But what puzzles even more, perhaps, the student of the Ṣūfi phenomenon, is the undoubted fact that the great Persian ecstatics are manifestly and overpoweringly mastered by a passionate and all-absorbing *love* for the supreme, divine beloved. It is this recognition of God as the unique object of *love* which is constantly borne upon one as the Ṣūfi's one and only way, and the emergence of this current of mystical love does not seem to have any discernible human or natural source. On the face of it, it might almost seem to spring from a new revelation, or, at any rate, from an ancient revelation, mysteriously and supernaturally renewed. Here one is reminded of Emile Dermenghem's remark that 'the original revelation was mystical as well as soteriological'.

But the mystery remains as to what or who was the immediate cause of its re-emergence.

A great deal has been written as to the possible origins of the Ṣūfi movement. Germs of it are, of course, to be found in the Qorān itself. It has also to be borne in mind that Islam had by this time spread over populations deeply impregnated by Christian teaching or Hellenistic (Neo-platonic) speculation. In Eastern Persia Buddhism had penetrated deeply, and as 'the Persians', according to the Prophet's well-known (and possibly apocryphal) saying, 'would journey to the Pleiades after knowledge', it is only to be expected that they would have had knowledge also of the Hindu sacred books. But when all this has been granted as a likelihood, or a quasi-certainty, it remains that the Ṣūfi phenomenon presents itself as a new, spontaneous and original flowering of religious feeling and intuition, and no one can put his finger on a single, incontrovertible author or originator of it. There is no single poet or mystic who can be said to be the prime mover in this revolution. The Ṣūfis themselves put it down to Mahomet himself, the divinely inspired embodiment of the perfect man. In doing this they probably aim at establishing their teaching in the heart of Mahometan orthodoxy. There are a certain number of passages in the Qorān which are susceptible of a mystical interpretation and which are the commonplaces of Islamic spiritual writers. A large number of other Qorānic texts are given a mystical interpretation by such writers, often in defiance of the plain, literal meaning of the passage quoted. In this respect, however, the Qorān is treated much in the same way as the Judaeo-Christian scriptures are treated by the early fathers and doctors. All take it for granted that the literal meaning contains an unlimited number of spiritual or mystical meanings, a mine which every spiritual man must penetrate and exploit for himself.

Although Plotinus is never quoted by name by the Ṣūfi writers, there cannot be the faintest doubt that his doctrines were known to them and came to be regarded by them as having almost the value of revealed truth. Writers like Sheikh Najm-edDin Rāzi (obiit A.D. 1256), in his *Mirṣād ul 'Ibād*, and

Sheikh Muhammad Lahiji Nūrbakhshi (obiit A.D. 1472), in his well-known Commentary on the *Gulshan i Rāz* of Shabistari, devote themselves at great length and with evident earnestness to expositions of the emanationist theories of the Neo-Platonist philosophers. Wide as was the diffusion of emanationist doctrines among the Ṣūfis, however, their necessary relation to the main Ṣūfi theses and trends is never very clear. The Ṣūfi is, above all, a lover and a spiritual guide. Rūmi is the supreme exponent of the Ṣūfi path, and his writings have only faint traces of emanationist speculation.

If we considered precisely the main trends and preoccupations of the Ṣūfis, we should be justified in concluding that, among external influences on their origins and development, Christianity, and especially Eastern Monasticism, was the chief and the most dynamic. At the time of the Islamic invasion, not only Syria but also Persia proper contained flourishing Christian communities. In Persia alone, at this period, there were as many as ninety monastic institutions. The Persian Church produced a number of remarkable teachers of theology and of the mystical life. One of the greatest of these was Babai the Great (A.D. 569–628), a wealthy Persian who had studied Persian (*Pahlevi*) literature before coming to Nisibis to study medicine. He became third abbot of the monastery on Mt Izla and was the foremost divine and theologian of the Nestorian Church at the crisis of its development. He wrote a commentary on the *Centuries* of Evagrius Ponticus, as well as *Rules for Novices and Canons for Monks*. Evagrius Ponticus himself, a pupil of Origen, Basil and Gregory, became a monk in the Scete Desert of Egypt and there composed in lapidary form his spiritual and mystical teaching. His works became the chief manual and the authoritative exposition of the ascetico-mystical life for Persian monachism. One or two quotations from his book *The Centuries* will serve to give some indication of the form of teaching which, through Persian monachism, may well have exercised a deep influence on the origins of Ṣūfism.

'A pure soul, next to God is God.'

'The naked mind is one that is perfect in the vision of itself and is held worthy of attaining to contemplation of the Holy Trinity.'

'He who has achieved pure prayer is God by grace.'

Although there can be no doubt that the loving, adoring, self-sacrificing figure of Jesus made an immeasurable impression on the peoples of the Near East, it is difficult to trace any scriptural or literary evidence of the propagation of Christian mystical teachings in Islamic mystical writers. References to the Last Supper and to the Crucifixion are not infrequent, but there is no sign of any precise or recognizable transmission of texts from, say, the Gospel of St John or the Epistles of St Paul. Any mystical influence of Christian origin seems to have been due to the example of monastic life and to the impact of Christian preoccupation with the pre-eminence of love in religion.

Buddhism, as mentioned above, had long flourished in Eastern Persia. It is generally assumed, both by European and Persian authors, that one of the predominant features of Ṣūfi mystical life, summed up in the word *fanā* (see Chapter VII) came in through Buddhist influence. This opinion is, no doubt, due to a comparison with the Buddhist doctrine of *nirvána*. But, apart from the fact that it is not certain that the concept of *nirvána* has been properly understood in the West, one must bear in mind that *fanā*—i.e. a passing away or transference of the personality—always aims at a state in which one lives in and for a higher personality, whether one's spiritual director or God Himself. This concept of *fanā* conforms more to the teaching of the *mahayána*, centred on the person of Amitabha, the saviour of the faithful, the Isvara who hears and answers the prayers of the world. Mahometan insistence on the transcendance of God seems to have guided the main stream of Persian mysticism and preserved it from mere subjectivism or Pantheism. Geographically as well as philosophically, Persia *stat in medio*.

However, the personality and example of the Buddha exercised an undoubted attraction on the Persian mind, and the story of one of the earliest Ṣūfis, Ibrahim ibn Adham, described as having been once King of Balkh, an Iranian outpost far out towards the borders of India, seems to be a legend based on the story of the Buddha himself. It is curious, too, that a very large number of notable Ṣūfi leaders arose in this north-eastern corner of Iran, now known as Khorasān, for it was in this region that Buddhism had flourished—not to speak of the great prophet of Ahura Mazda, Zoroaster. The north-eastern provinces, indeed, were the scene of an intense cosmopolitan life in which Greek or Hellenized elements mingled with Iranian and partially Iranified Central Asiatic elements. They represented, it has been said, a central crucible between the West and India. Buddhism certainly flourished in these regions, but it was chiefly in its newer form as *mahayána*, the 'Great Vehicle', that it spread towards Irán. Ultimately, however, Irán set a barrier to any further expansion of Buddhism towards the West. It set out, therefore, towards the East, carrying with it certain notions borrowed from Irán: its Messianic dreams, its paradise, its cult of the sun and of light, its mystical cosmogony. The French excavations carried out in Afghanistán since 1920 have revealed plastic arts betokening Iranobuddhist inspiration.

All this happened contemporaneously with the religious reform attempted in Irán by Máni. Máni, a Persian by race, was born at Babylon about A.D. 215. His aim was to found a comprehensive religion reconciling the doctrines of Zoroaster, Buddha and Jesus Christ. He inaugurated his public life by a journey in India, at the time when the Sassanian Shahpur was conducting a lightning campaign in the valley of the Indus. Some writers have even stated that Máni took part in Sháhpur's campaign, between A.D. 256 and 260, against Valerian, and that he then met Plotinus, who was serving as a soldier in the Roman army.

I mention these facts simply to give some idea of the extent to which Persia, in the period preceding the Islamic invasion, had been subject to fertilization and cross-fertilization by religions and philosophies which contained a strong mystical element. If this was so, the reason is to be found in the attraction which such doctrines possessed for the Persian mind and their keenness in religious speculation.

One consequence of these cross-fertilizations was that, many centuries later, Indian gurus and swámis recognized in the Ṣūfis and dervishes who came from Persia in the wake of conquering Islamic armies co-religionists who had the same mystical preoccupations as themselves. The Persian *Pir u Murshid* fitted easily into the spiritual scheme of things in India and would often be consulted by Hindu inquirers.

In the years following the Mahometan conquests, the newly-founded city of Kūfa, in southern Iraq, became, in its turn, a nursery-ground of idealist, Neo-Platonist and Christian-Hellenic doctrines and tendencies and, at the same time, a forcing-ground of the pro-'Ali Shi'a, closely allied to a specifically Persian outlook. It is easy to understand, therefore, that Kufa also gave birth to some of the earliest Ṣūfis.

These early Ṣūfis, as we saw, had little concern for mystical themes as such. Their dominant aim was to flee the deceitful and corrupting world and to devote themselves in silence and solitude, to practices of austerity, fasting and other forms of ascetical discipline. Their outlook was of that simple and elementary sort which accords with the Arabo-Mahometan religion in which they had been brought up.

The earliest of these arose in the south of Iraq. Such were Hassan of Basrah and Abu Hashim of Kufa, this latter, apparently the first to whom the soubriquet of Ṣūfi was given. This region had been worked over by Zoroastrian and then by Christian influences during the epoch of the Sassanian monarchs. Basra also produced the remarkable woman Saint and mystic, Rabi'a al 'Adawiyya, who died in A.D. 801.

But the diffusion of ideas was very rapid in Islām which, in its early and expanding centuries, was unhampered by strict national frontiers and barriers. Thus the Ṣūfi Movement soon spread like wildfire over the whole Islamic scene. Gradually, too, it began to develop doctrinally and to be transformed from within, by subtle but rapid stages, into a lofty and coherent mystical system.

When we speak of 'diffusion' here, we must not let ourselves imagine that such things happen automatically. The diffusion of mystical doctrines in Islám was the work of certain great and influential individuals whose reputation drew inquirers to them from afar.

These inquirers, formed in the school of a great sheikh, a *Pir u Murshid* (spiritual father and guide), propagated his teaching, became spiritual Masters in their turn, formed other disciples, and so collaborated in the formation of a spiritual chain (silsileh), the personages forming which are often enumerated in detail. This living chain of religious teachers is an essential feature in the Ṣūfi scheme of things. Surviving links of these chains must now be exceeding few, save perhaps where a surviving religious Order has managed to ensure a continuance of doctrine. In the absence of notable teachers, however, a far from negligible norm and witness of the traditional teaching is provided by authoritative books such as the *Maṣnavi*, the *Gulshan i Rāz* and so forth. In many cases, too, witnesses to the continuity of mystical teaching are to hand in the shape of later Commentators. One such, in the case of the *Gulshan i Rāz*, is the well-known Lāhiji Nūrbakhshi, who wrote in A.D. 1472.

In this study I wish to concentrate attention on the sounder elements of Persian mystical teaching, but one need not therefore be blind to other elements which may rightly be regarded as divagations and deformations, or, at any rate, as exaggerations of a disconcerting or even repulsive nature. Such elements have not been wanting in Ṣūfism. The Ṣūfi teaching does not, of right, possess within itself a guarantee of infallibility. As a manifestation of spiritual life within the Islamic community, it shares the weakness inherent in Islám itself, a weakness inherited from its Mahometan source and due also to the lack of a living infallible authority in the Islamic body. This lack of an external authority has meant that the Ṣūfis could look upon themselves as a law unto themselves. Ghazāli made a notable effort to establish Ṣūfism solidly within the boundaries of Moslem orthodoxy, whatever that may be. But the Ṣūfi, at heart, does not consider himself bound by the legislation of the *ahl i ẓāhir* (externalists). It is an accepted principle among them that *lā fiṣṣufiyya kalāmun*—'there is no formal (scholastic) theology in Ṣūfism'. Ṣūfism, for better or for worse, is a doctrine derived from inspiration, contemplation and experience, and not a system deduced from positive Islamic theology. The Ṣūfi teacher willingly makes use of theological statements, but his treatment and interpretation of them always goes beyond them, in what he considers to be the pure, spiritual sense. That, indeed, may be said to be the fundamental preoccupation and purpose of Ṣūfism. Ṣūfi teachers express unbounded respect for the utterances of the Prophet, but that is chiefly because they assume him to have been the recipient of mystical communications as well as of divine revelations granted to him as founder of a world religion. In a sense, they show a deeper sense of responsibility towards the Moslem faith than do the *mutakallimin* (positive theologians), inasmuch as they are most earnestly concerned to warn the faithful against the dangers of a merely external performance of their religious duties and a merely parrot-like repetition of what has been taught them. It is not surprising, therefore, that it was above all in Persia that the principle of *ijtihād*, or duty of individual investigation and interpretation of religious truth, was initiated and maintained.

It is clear, then, that the Ṣūfis did not wish to originate a new religion (*maẓhab*). They were not even concerned to take up any precise position towards the Sunni-Shi'a controversy. Many of the early Ṣūfis were actually Sunnis. This may have been because questions about external authority or legitimacy did not arouse their interest. But they all shared in a quite distinct spiritual climate and had a very genuine *esprit de corps*. There was no visible hierarchy among them, although many believed in the existence of an invisible hierarchy, under whose supreme head, the *Quṭb* (pole or pivot), other *Awliyā* ('saints'), in their different ranks and degrees, kept up the spiritual order of the universe.

Whether in the Ghaib (invisible world) or in the visible world, there was no formal authority other than that of spiritual distinction and experience. Authority of some kind however, there must be. The wayfarer who would take no advice and submit to no training was condemned. The first essential was to place oneself under the direction of a *Pir u Murshid* and to obey him blindly and implicitly. Some of the greatest mystics of the way served thus an exacting apprenticeship over a long period of years. When certain inspired mystics had consigned their teaching to writing, whether in prose or verse, their books often served as manuals. For the Niʻmatullāhis of Persia, Shabistari's *Gulshan i Rāz* served (and perhaps still serves) as traditional manual for all those men or women (instructed in separate groups) who came under their direction in a kind of 'Third Order', meeting once a week in the evening, that is, when their daily avocations were finished. In the days before the Turks were expelled from Crete, one could, from the courtyard of a *Tekyeh* watch the rhythmic swaying of the white-robed members of the Mevlevi Confraternity into whose circle, at last, the professional Mevlevi Dervish came to perform his own central gyration, as a sun amid the planets, all (as a young supporter whispered to the invited guests) having no other meaning than the love of God.

The Ṣūfi movement, indeed, was nothing if not a movement of self-abandonment to the divine beloved. The founder of the Mevlevis, Jalālu' ddin Rūmi, was a remarkable soul, inspired if ever man was inspired, majdhūb (drawn, attracted by grace) if ever man was drawn in this way. But of his disciples, though a number, no doubt, caught something of his fire and élan, many more found it easier to repeat the movements than to recapture the first, fine, careless rapture.

Such, for better or for worse, is the Ṣūfi. It should be added —it will appear clearly inevitable after what has been said— that he roundly condemned high and dry intellectualism and the narrow Semitic formalism and rationalism which was the bane of the Mahometan theological schools. This contempt for shortsighted 'reason' often comes out in the poetry of the Ṣūfi school. Hāfiẓ gives it its highest and most caustic expression. In one place he says: (*Ay ki az daftar i 'aql*, etc.) 'Oh thou who art trying to learn the marvel of love from the copybook of reason (*taql*), I am very much afraid that you will never really see the point.'

So, too, in another place Ḥāfiẓ exclaims:

'Rub out everything you have copied into your exercise book, if you would be my fellow-learner, for the science of love is not to be found in books.'

Beyond dry-as-dust reason, then, the Ṣūfi seeks, through a transformation of the heart in love, to win a higher form of knowledge, a kind of direct vision of reality, that divine reality which transcends the sphere of the senses and of concepts based on sense perception. It is here, of course, that we begin to see his approach to the Neo-Platonic outlook.

By a strange paradox, however, and, indeed, through the very necessity of the case, the Ṣūfi apostle makes use of the most vivid and abundant vocabulary of symbolism drawn from the language of human love. His object was to make it clear that the divine beloved deserved a love and a devotion at least as fervent and passionate as could be those inspired by a human object. He resorted to this method, too, because he aimed at winning over, not only the learned, but the whole population, down to the least cultured among them. The results of this can be seen in the Persian people to this day. A certain mystical culture is common among them and all of them take a genuine pleasure in discussing such themes. The westerner will often be astonished to find an illiterate peasant making an apt quotation from a mystical poem. Thus, if the Ṣūfi made such abundant use of poetry, it was because he knew how sensitive were the peoples of eastern Islamic countries to the influence of a poetical medium. To express a truth in a telling poetical phrase was more than half the battle.

There were also other reasons for this use of poetry. One of these was the greater security the Ṣūfi mystic felt when he had clothed his teaching, which might easily be liable to the accusation of heresy, in the ambiguous and, for the positive theologian, usually undecipherable language of poetry and metaphor. It was a form of *ketmān* (deliberate concealment).

Then again, the message of the Ṣūfi was a message of love and divine passion, of which poetry seems to be the natural expression. If he endeavoured to lend his poetry every possible charm and beauty, this was also with a view to rendering it less unworthy of its real, divine Object. As an Arabic saying has it: 'God is beautiful and cannot but love beauty.'

While, then, the Ṣūfis made no attempt to appeal mainly to a philosophical élite, as was the tendency with the Neo-Platonists, nor to constitute a sort of esoteric Inner Circle, like the 'elect' of the Manichees, it was inevitable that, as time went on, a specialized vocabulary of mystical terms should be evolved. There is nothing official about these terms, but most Ṣūfis are agreed as to their acceptation. Similarly, all the mystical poets share a common repertory of apparently erotic expressions on whose interpretation, likewise, they are agreed. Such are, for instance, the mole or beauty-spot of the beloved, her dark tresses, her curls and so on. These expressions remind us at once of similar ones often quoted from the Song of Songs by Christian mystics. There are, too, traditional images of the seemingly hopeless love of a human heart for the divine being, such as that of the love-sick Nightingale and the rose, the moth and the candle, Majnūn and Leila. Similar themes are illustrated by comparison with Qorānic personages such as Joseph (*Yūsuf*) and Zuleikhā (the name given in the Qorān to Potiphar's wife), a pair commonly chosen to represent an impossible love-romance, Joseph, in this case, standing for the transcendant and unattainable beloved.

Figures drawn from Iranian mythology, such as Shirin and Farhād, are less frequently introduced as mystical symbols.

THREE

THE WAY AND ITS GOAL

THE Ṣūfis spoke of themselves as travellers or wayfarers, faring upon a way (*rāh, ṭariqa*) which was staked out, but on which, nevertheless, a guide, in the person of an experienced spiritual man, a *Pir u Murshid,* was indispensable.

This way led the traveller away from self—to begin with, from the carnal, self-indulgent self, and then, more and more, from any assertion of self or conscious regard of self.

The goal or destination is defined in various ways: as *ma'rifat,* or gnosis, or as union with God (*vuṣūl, viṣāl, ittiḥād*), as vision of Him, in His unveiled beauty and glory, or again, as utter consumption in the fire of love, or, simply, as perfection. The gist of the matter seems to be deliverance from self by the alchemy of divine love, which takes a man out of himself and prompts him to consider himself as the servant of all.

As Khōja Ḥāfiz says: 'Any *qibla* (i.e. any direction or intention of prayer or life) is better than self-worship'.

For the great mystics, however, if self-regard is the great enemy, it is because it is the chief veil or film over the mirror of the soul, shutting out the vision of the one, true beloved, who ought, even now, to fill the lover's consciousness, so that he can say, with Ḥāfiẓ,

'So full is my soul's horizon of the beloved,
'All thought of self has gone from my mind.'

In a later chapter we shall see more in detail the implications of this 'loss of self' (*fanā*). Meanwhile, amid the painful stages of the Way, the pilgrim is still taken up with the seemingly endless task of escaping from and subjugating the 'nafs', or carnal self, negotiating the purgative way before he can hope to climb to the heights of illumination and the summit of union. A Ṣūfi poet tells us:

'On the hat of Poverty three renouncements are inscribed:
'Quit this world, quit the next world, quit quitting.'

By these last cryptic words is meant the need to cut off all reflection on, and satisfaction in, the thought of having renounced anything. That would vitiate renouncement, being a sign that the disciple, having put his hand to the plough, is looking back on himself, his own merits and achievements. To seek anything other than the one beloved, whether it be rewards or pleasures, angels, houris, paradise, let alone honour and esteem in this world, is idolatry and polytheism. Here the mystic is in full accord with the dominant spirituality of the Qorān, interpreted with his own, subtle, psychological insight.

It is, therefore, the powerful attraction of the eternal beauty which, in the last resort, draws the lover away from all else, including himself. But as the traveller on this way finds himself faced by all kinds of difficulties, the masters of the path have come to his help by designating an ordered series of 'stages' (*maqāmāt, marāḥil*), through which he must strive to pass, in due order. The *Kitāb ul Luma* of Abū Naṣr al-Sarrāj, in common with the majority of writings on the subject, enumerates seven of these stages: conversion or repentance; fear of the Lord; renunciation; poverty; endurance; trust in God; contentment (*riḍā*)—the state of one who pleases God and is always pleased with Him and His ways.

These seven stages are to be reached by the personal endeavours of the disciple, although the constant need of divine grace is presupposed in each case. They are said, therefore, to be acquired (*kasbi, iktisābi*) and are not characterized, as are the *aḥwāl*, by purely supernatural infusion. They are due to *kūshish* (effort) and not to *kashish* (supernatural attraction). They are in the line of *mujāhada* (striving) and not of *mushāhada* (contemplation). They represent what the Prophet, in a well-known saying, referred to as the 'major holy war' (*al jihād al akbar*), far more important and meritorious, therefore, than merely fighting the infidel outside. In the language of our own spiritual writers, these stages make up the *Via purgativa*. Their purpose is to set the disciple free from the trammels of the self, to dispose the soul to self-denial, self-transcendance, self-surrender. From another angle they may be said to aim at a progressive purification of the soul, a testing and training in purity of intention *ikhlās, takhlis*). In this way the *sālik* learns to eliminate all *gharaḍ* (ulterior motives). God Himself helps in this by sending him mysterious afflictions, manoeuvring him, as it were, into voluntary death (*maut i ikhtiāri*). He learns thus to be perfectly supple and pliable in the hands of God—one writer says: 'like a corpse', anticipating St Ignatius.

By all these methods the spiritual athlete wears down the veils or films which interfere with the immediate play of the breath of divine grace. His efforts in this sense cannot of themselves acquire supernatural graces of contemplation,but they serve to lay his soul bare to such influences and attractions and are, as it were, his own mute pleadings for them.

It is interesting to trace, more especially in the earlier masters of the way, the close connection they saw between the practice of self-denial and penance and the attainment of the mystical goal. Sheikh 'Aṭṭār, in his *Tazkirat al 'Awliyā* records the answers of a number of leading mystics to the question: What is a Ṣūfi?

One of the earliest of these is Junayd of Baghdād (d. A.D. 910). He is known as one of the moderate type of Ṣūfi, a 'sober' mystic as distinguished from an 'intoxicated' one, like Bāyazid Bisṭāmi, of a previous generation.

Junayd says that Ṣūfism consists in this, that the Lord causes you to die to yourself and to live in Him.

In another place he writes: 'The *'árif* (gnostic or contemplative) is one from the depths of whose consciousness (*sirr*) God speaks, while he himself is silent.

Again: 'Ṣūfism is a steep ascent, allowing of no peace or rest.'

Abu 'l Hussein Nuri said: 'The Ṣūfi is one who keeps hold of nothing and is held and bound by nothing.'

Abu Said of Mihneh (d. 1049), one of the most original of the early Persian mystics, once said: 'To be a Ṣūfi is to give up all worries and there is no worse worry than your self (literally, your you-ness). When occupied with self, you are separated from God. The way to God is but one step: the step out of yourself. He that knows himself (i.e. as non-existent) knows his Lord[1] (i.e. as the self-subsistent being).'

It is not difficult, of course, to find similar teaching in the works of Christian mystics. Thus, in the *Cloud of Unknowing* (Ch. 43), we find:

> 'Thou shalt understand that thou shalt not only in this work forget all other creatures than thyself . . . but also thou shalt forget thyself. For thou shalt find, when thou hast forgotten all other creatures and all their works—yea! and also all thine own works—that there shall remain yet after, betwixt thee and thy God, a naked knowing and a feeling of thy own being, which must always be destroyed if thou art to feel verily the perfection of this work.'

So, too, in the life of St Catherine of Siena it is recorded that Jesus once said to her: 'I am He who is. Thou art she who is not.'

Shihāb ed Din Suhravardi, founder of the Suhravardia Order, in his *Awārif al Ma'ārif* (Mystical Scholars), begins by distinguishing the *zāhid* (ascete) and the *faqir* (mendicant, poverello) from the Ṣūfi as such. The Ṣūfi includes, in an eminent way, the ascete and the faqir, but the converse is not the case. After he has reviewed a large number of definitions of Ṣūfism, as given by leading mystics, his conclusion is that, taken all in all, Ṣūfism is worship of God based on love (*maḥabbat*). The Ṣūfi views the relation between the Creator and the creature as that of a lover and the beloved. Here we stumble across a difficulty of vocabulary. The terms favoured by Ṣūfis corresponding to 'lover and beloved' are *Áshiq u Ma'shūq*', while love, in this connection, is *'ishq*. Now *'ishq*, a word of Arabic origin, of course, is more particularly used of *l'amour passion*. Hence the Hanbalite theologian, Ibn al Jauzi, and others of his way of mind, take objection to the word as applied to God, on the grounds that it can only signify sexual

[1] Reference to the well-known ḥadith: *Man 'arafa nafsahu, 'arafa rabbahu.* (Who knows himself, knows his Lord.)

love of a fleshly nature. We can see here, in the Moslem world, a counterpart to the objection raised by Christian theologians to the Greek *eros* or the Latin *amor* as equivalents to the Pauline *agape*. In reality, of course, divine love transcends all human notions of love. If the Ṣūfis chose to use *ishq* rather than *maḥabbat* (a pity they didn't think of *mihr*, a pure Persian word!), it was because they wished to stress the fact that we must attribute to His love for the contemplative soul and to that soul's love for Him, *at least* as much fire and fervour as we are accustomed to associate with passionate love between the sexes. The Ṣūfis, in their wayward, rapturous way, succeeded in imposing these terms, however shocking they may have seemed to the old-fashioned, and no-one would ever now dream of calling them in question.

The seven stages (*maqāmāt*) defined by Abū Nasr al-Sarrāj, enumerated earlier in this chapter, represent the ascetical and moral demands made upon any sincere seeker for truth and perfection. The thesis is, that each of these stages must be attained in due order before proceeding to the next. Much of what the Ṣūfis write on the virtues for which the seeker should strive would with us be considered to form part of a normal moral and religious education, with no necessary bearing on mystical life. This fact reflects, no doubt, some grave deficiencies which are apt to show themselves in the day to day teaching of Islám. At the same time, when we find ourselves disagreeably affected by the free and easy utterances and conduct of some of the less 'sober' of the Ṣūfis, it is reassuring to note that the really responsible Masters of the Ṣūfi way inculcate so rigorous a moral and ascetical training for those who aspire after the heights of contemplation. In this the writers do but set down in black and white what was the invariable method of the *Pir u Murshid* (spiritual director) under whom the disciple set out upon the Way and to whom he had to vow the most perfect and unquestioning obedience.

The disciple (*murid*) was expected to entertain towards his *Murshid* or Sheikh sentiments of devotion amounting to a sort of cult. He was to merge his personality in that of the Sheikh (*fanā fil-sheikh*) who, for him, was the one mediator with an otherwise inaccessible divinity. In this the Ṣūfis depart from the strict line of Islamic orthodoxy, which does not recognize any mediation between the individual believer and his God. Not even Mahomet (or should we say, Mahomet least of all?) claimed any such mediatorial role. In spite of this, the evolution of Neo-Platonic thought in the Ṣūfi theosophy led to his being awarded a position in the spiritual hierarchy of beings practically equivalent to that of the Logos. Under this aspect he is known as the 'Mahomet-Light' and ranks among humans as the perfect man (*al insānul kāmil*), the supreme exemplar and purpose of creation. The installation of the Sheikh in his pivotal place in the Ṣūfi system owes a great deal, almost certainly, to the living example of the Christian monastic organization which, in the East, at any rate, turns to a large extent on the spiritual authority of the saintly Father Abbot-Apa in Egypt. The indispensable need of a spiritual father and director has always been insisted on in the Greek Church. In the West this feature has tended to be replaced by the cautionary safeguards of a fixed and approved rule.

The Murshid or Sheikh, however, whatever the degree of his authority and influence, had had, first of all, to submit himself to a long training in accordance with the principles of a mystico-ascetical path the outlines of which became clearer and firmer as time went on. Only a very great personality could raise a profitable originality above the wise normality of such a body of doctrine.

The fixed *maqāmāt* and *aḥwāl* on the Ṣūfi way are examples of this crystallization. Not that all mystical writers conform inevitably to the positive standards of Abū Naṣr or of Hujviri. Thus a poet like Sheikh 'Aṭṭār, in his *Mantiq utTair* (Language of Birds) enumerates the stages on the course of the birds to their mystical goal as follows:

> 'There are seven valleys on the way. When you have passed through these seven valleys, you reach the Presence Chamber. . . . The first valley is questing and seeking. Next to it is the vale of Love; then the vale of Knowledge (*ma'rifat* or *gnosis*). The fourth is detachment and liberty of heart

(*istighnā*). The fifth pure unification (*tawḥid*). The sixth, grievous bewilderment. The seventh, Poverty and utter loss of self (*fanā*). After that valley there is no more deliberate advance: going is forgone, henceforth one is *drawn*.'

It will be seen that Sheikh 'Aṭṭār here, with the freedom of the inspired mystic and poet, submerges and mingles stages and states, replaces fear of the Lord and renouncement by *istighnā* (utter independence of created things) and brackets together the stage of Poverty with the mystic depths of *fanā*. In this he well illustrates the characteristic urgency of the inspired mystic, eager to ensure the primacy of love and abandonment of self and impatient to yield up human efforts to the immensely faster and more efficacious attractions of supernatural grace. Other authors show a like urgency and impatience where repentance is concerned. Should sins be called to mind? The answer is, that if repentance is due to the stirrings of a sincere love of God, then this love will submerge and blot out all remembrance of sin in favour of remembrance of the one beloved.

In like manner, where poverty is concerned, the Ṣūfi masters at once begin to effervesce with indignation at the thought that a true lover could ever be content with renunciation of a few earthly belongings. No! If true love be there, it will urge the lover to go out to the beloved beyond all created things, not least his own self, beyond this world and the next.

We must therefore bear in mind that the 'stages', although by definition they lie in the sphere of acquisition and effort, must constantly be interpreted in the light of the mystic's supreme concerns. Their materiality is constantly bathed in effusions of grace and longing. Grace, which is their ultimate motive, cannot be hindered by any scholastic formula from infiltrating into the bony structure of asceticism. Once this is understood, it can be readily admitted that defined 'stages' are a handy means of finding one's way among the fluid intricacies of the soul's progress. Are they rigorously confined to the seven enumerated by al-Sarrāj? Clearly not. Since we are dealing with human souls, with their infinite variety, the number might easily be multiplied to seventy times seven. But, as with the gifts of the Holy Ghost, it is a matter of practical convenience to assume that they are seven. Others, however numerous, can group themselves under these heads.

FOUR

THE SEVEN STAGES

I. REPENTANCE OR CONVERSION

THE first stage on the way, then, is *tawba*—repentance or conversion. This, like any other spiritual blessing, is a sheer gift of grace (*'aṭā maḥẓ*). At the same time, unlike the 'states', it is put within the reach of every man or woman and involves his or her co-operation. It means turning one's back on worldly vanities, realizing that the world is a 'rotting carcase' and that self is a fickle support. So the soul, awakened from its dream world of carelessness and neglect (*ghiflat*), begins to advance towards God and perfection and away from the snares and baits of created pleasures. The Qorān itself is full of such instigations.

Books like the *Taẓkirat al Awliyā* abound in stories of striking and miraculous conversions. That of Bāyazid Bisṭāmi may be related as an example. Sheikh 'Aṭṭār tells how Bāyazid's mother sent him to school at Bisṭām. One day the class came to the *sūra Loqmān* in the Qorān (No. 31) and to the verse: 'Be thankful to me and to thy parents.' The master explained the meaning of this passage. As he listened, Bāyazid felt his mind strongly worked upon. He put down his slate and asked for permission to go home and say something to his mother. Receiving the permission, he went home. His mother cried: You little vagabond, what brings you here? Have you had a present or been given a holiday? He replied: No. I have come to a verse in the Qorān in which God bids me serve Him and serve you. I can't manage to serve in two houses at once. I can't get away from that verse. Either ask me from God so that I may be all yours, or put me in the service of God so that I may be entirely with Him.

His mother said: I put you in God's service and set you free to do as you see fit. Go and belong to God.

Bāyazid left Bisṭām and practised the ascetical life in Syria for thirty years.

The penitent longs to make good his defects and satisfy his great needs, but, left to himself, he knows not where to turn. He has then to seek out a teacher, a *Pir u Murshid*, who will tell him what to do and guide him on the way of perfection. Thus he sets out on his great quest. God's grace is abounding, but the condition for profiting by it is to seek it. Ḥāfiz says: 'Love's physician has the healing breath of Jesus Himself and is full of compassion; but if He find no pain in you, how will He administer a remedy?' And regarding the spirit of searching and seeking Maulānā Rūmi, in the third book of the *Maṣnavi*, says:

'In whatever state you may be, keep on the search!
'Thou dry-lipped one, ever be on the search for Water!
'That dry lip of thine is a sure token
'That in the end it will find the source.
'This seeking is a blessed restlessness,
'It overcomes every obstacle and is the key to thy desires.
'Though thou have no vessel, fail not to seek:
'On the way of God no vessel is required.
'Whatever goods and skills you may possess
'Were they not, to begin with, a quest, a thought?
'No, Sir, cease not one moment from thy search
'And you will find, oh wonder, whatever you desire.
'Sooner or later he who seeks becomes he who finds,
'Since ever he is hastening to serve.'

2. FEAR OF THE LORD (WARA')

The *second stage* which the convert must aim at and which is, as it were, necessarily called for by the first, is *wara'*, which may be translated as 'fear of the Lord'. A similar position is given to it by St Augustine and St Thomas in their exposition of the gifts of the Holy Ghost. Bishr Ḥāfi, a well-known ascetical writer, explains it as 'avoidance of whatever has the least semblance or suspicion of wrong and a ceaseless watch over the heart'. In the case of this virtue, as with others, the Ṣūfi teachers contrast the fear of God shown by the *ahl i ẓāhir*, or externalists, with that felt by the *ahl i dil* or men of enlightenment, or again by the gnostic who enjoys union with God. The last-named, as Abū Suleimān Dārāni says, detests whatever hinders the heart from attention to God. In the same strain Hakīm Sanāi of Ghazna writes:

> If a thing hold you back on the Way, what matter if it be faith or infidelity?
> If it keeps you far from the Friend, what matter if the image be foul or fair?

3. DETACHMENT (ZUHD)

Fear of the Lord leads necessarily to the *third stage, zuhd*, which can be translated as detachment or renouncement of the world in order to give oneself to God. The Ṣūfi regards attachment to this world as the source of all sin and quitting the world as the source of every good. This detachment must not be a merely external thing. It must be a genuine detachment of the heart. The Ṣūfi warns against the danger of hypocrisy, of becoming a worshipper of outward appearances (*zāhid i ẓāhirparast*). This warning has bitten deep into the Persian soul. Through fear of hypocrisy the educated classes hesitate to practise their religion in public and this bashfulness has become almost an inhibition.

But the *ẓāhid* whose actions are guided by the great principles of the Way is one who 'has passed through the seven cities of love beyond every consideration of being and non-being'. He is detached even from his detachment and, being occupied with God alone, pays no heed to the world and its passing show.

This feature of the path is, of course, found among Christians likewise. But in the case of the Persians there is no doubt that they saw a strong inducement to such a life of renouncement in the succession of shattering calamities which ruined their country and jeopardized life and property. It is a feature of

Ṣūfism which commends itself less to Persians of today, who are anxious to encourage thrift and enterprise. It certainly suits the circumstances of the Islamic period of Persian history more than the grandeurs of the pure Persian dynasties.

4. POVERTY (FAQR)

By easy stages the *sālik* (traveller, pilgrim) now reaches the important stage of poverty (*faqr*), which, it is easy to see, follows logically upon those that preceded it, may, indeed, be looked upon as their fuller flowering or explicitation.

Voluntary poverty is the Ṣūfi's pride, as it was the pride of Mahomet: not, of course, that the mere absence of riches or worldly goods is of any value in itself. The Ṣūfi voluntarily dismisses these things in order to prove his independence of them and his reliance on God alone—or rather, apart from wishing to prove anything, he is lifted away from earthly possessions and attachments by the purity and fervour of his love for God. Among the earlier ascetes of predominantly Arab stock, this eagerness to be rid of all beside God was, no doubt, connected with a certain fanatical and exaggerated notion of predestination and of the consequent vanity of human efforts and the superfluousness of secondary causes. But as Ṣūfism grew to take on a more mystical and ecstatic note, such notions were outpassed. Love became the guiding motive and poverty was but the sign of the mystic's absorption in and care for the one beloved. Henceforth it was not the mere absence of riches that mattered, but rather the loss of any desire for them or attachment to them. The vacant heart was more important than the vacant hand. A man might thus be a faqir at heart even while living in the midst of affluence and in a position of worldly dignity. Ḥāfiẓ, referring clearly to Jalālud Din Tūrān-shāh, Vizir of Shāh Shujā', wrote:

> 'I humbly bow to the Asaph[1] of the age
> 'Who has the outward show of lordship and the inner spirit of a dervish.'

[1] Asaph was the Vizir of King Solomon.

In fact, when the true inwardness of the Ṣūfi notion of poverty is ascertained, it is found to be concerned rather with self-renouncement, or self-denial, in the sense that the true lover has no thought for himself, considers himself as non-existent: the being of the beloved is all that matters. When the being that might have laid claim to ownership of worldly goods is no longer there, poverty is transcended. So *idhā tamma'l faqr, fahwallāh.*—'Where poverty is complete, there is God.'

This utter detachment from created things produces a state of bewilderment (*taḥayyur*), to use the customary term. The Ṣūfi who has been drawn away (*majdhūb*) from all earthly cares is said to be *bi sar u pā*—without head or foot. In this state he may show signs of becoming indifferent to human opinion or blame—a *malāmati*. He will even prefer to be blamed and decried, in order that his true mystical state may be concealed from the vulgar.

With his selfhood thus renounced and outpassed, he no longer has any motive or desire for choosing. He chooses neither poverty nor wealth. His one preference is for what God sends or bestows. So, too, he does not (as Suhravardi says) renounce temporal things for the sake of something to be received in exchange (such as the joys of paradise, the company of houris, etc.), but for the sake of actual states (*aḥwāl maujūda*). He is *ibn waqtihi*—that is, he lives in the present moment, not for the future. As Rūmi says, 'In the vocabulary of the Way you do not find the word tomorrow'. It is by this token, above all, that the purity of the Ṣūfi's motives is tested and also the purity of his faith. To seek something other than God is a form of godlessness or idolatry. For him, even the ritual ablutions have value only insofar as they symbolize the worshipper's detachment from the least speck of created things.

The true inwardness of poverty as a dominant feature in the Ṣūfi mystical system is excellently summed up by Molla Abdur-Raḥmān Jāmi in the opening pages of his collection of Ṣūfi biographies called *Nafaḥātul Uns* (Perfumes of Fellowship). Jāmi, both as a mystic and as a poet, writing in the fifteenth century of our era, may be said himself to sum up the mystical and poetic achievements of his predecessors. The essential passages of his exposition are here translated and somewhat abridged.

'As regards the "poor" (*fuqarā*), they are those who own none of the resources and riches of this world and, in their search for the grace and good pleasure of God, have renounced everything. Their motive is one of three things:

'(1) The hope of lightening the account they will have to render and the fear of future punishment.

'(2) Expectation of abundant merit and of an earlier entrance into Heaven, since "the poor enter Paradise five hundred years before the rich".[1]

'(3) Finding assurance and tranquility of conscience owing to their frequent performance of good deeds, to which they give undivided attention.

'The faqir differs from the *malāmati* (one who defies opinion) and from the self-styled Ṣūfi (*mutaṣawwif*) in that they seek for paradise and their own souls' pleasure, whereas he seeks God alone and a closer walk with Him. The Ṣūfi, again, ranks higher than the faqir as such, since his state includes and eminently surpasses what the faqir aims at. The Ṣūfi jumps, as one might say, all the requirements and conditions for entering the stage of poverty. He takes to himself the rare bloom and lustre of every stage that he outpasses and gives it the special tint of his own rank. In the Ṣūfi, poverty takes on a higher quality, in that he declines to attribute to his own merits any of his actions, states and stages, lays no personal claim to them, regards none of them as belonging to himself or exclusive to himself. He does not regard himself at all. He no longer has any existence, essence or attributes. He is utterly self-denied and self-effaced. This is the inner reality of poverty. The rest is only the external mark or mode of it.

'The *faqir* is veiled (from God) by his choice of poverty and by the resulting comfort he finds for his spirit, whereas the Ṣūfi has no particular desire. All his will and desire is swallowed up in the will and desire of God.'

[1] Saying attributed to Mahomet.

5. PATIENCE

The stage that follows immediately and logically upon the stage of poverty is *ṣabr*, which can be translated as patience, steadfastness or perseverance. This virtue, without which the depths of poverty could not be borne, is said to be the better part of faith, if not the whole of it. Where true love of God is found and the sense of His providential ways understood, the 'slings and arrows of outrageous fortune' are not merely borne, but are accepted with ease and pleasure, as manifesting the will of God. The secret of perfect patience is in this, that the trials and afflictions of life are met, not merely *in* God and *with* God, but actually *by means of* God Himself.

Junayd declared that 'the perfection of patience is resignation' (*tawakkul*).

The seeker after God and perfection needs this virtue of patience in an exceptional degree, since, in the hope of noble results, God will submit His servant to severe testing (*imtiḥān*). The life of one who seeks God alone is usually marked by many afflictions and losses. It will be one mass of ruins—the ruins of all earthly hopes and vanities. Even without these outward devastations, the life of the mystic is an ocean of sorrow: and this sorrow he would not exchange for all the world's joys, since it springs from his acute sense of separation from the true, divine beloved and from all that constitutes the true happiness and peace of his heart. It is an incurable pain and, like the mystic's poverty, this too is his pride. Moreover, the afflictions of the saint are a blessing in disguise, since it is by them that God conceals his true glory from the eyes of the profane.

The trial and testing of things is an essential part of the world-process, whether in bodies or in souls. In the second book of the *Maṣnavi*, in a passage headed 'On making trial of everything, so that the good and evil which are in it may be brought to view', Jalālu' ddin Rūmi, after describing how the earth is brought, by an alternation of kind treatment (spring and summer) and harshness (autumn and winter), to show what treasures it has robbed and hidden, says, regarding interior trials, 'He that wages the warfare of the spirit now enjoys expansion of heart, now endures oppression, pain and torment . . . all for the sake of the soul's coin being brought into sight and use. Truth and falsehood have been mingled and good and bad coin have been poured into the travelling-bag. Therefore they need a picked touchstone, one that has undergone many tests in assaying realities.'

In the fourth book of the *Maṣnavi* (vv. 90–100) Rūmi shows how the evil met with in this world has the effect of turning men back to God: 'The servant of God complains to Him of pain and smart. God replies, "After all, grief and pain have made thee humbly entreating and righteous. You should make complaint rather of the bounty that befalls thee and removes thee far from my door and makes thee an outcast." He continues: "There is an animal called the porcupine. It is made stout and big by blows of the stick. The more you cudgel it, the more it thrives. Assuredly the true believer's soul is a porcupine, for it is made fat and stout by the blows of tribulation. For this reason the tribulation and abasement laid upon the prophets is greater than that laid upon all other creatures in the world, so that their souls became stouter. If then you will not mortify yourself, accept at least the tribulations God gives you without choice on your part, for affliction sent by the friend is the means of your purification".'

The *gham i dūst*, or grieving for the absent beloved, is a note which often recurs in Persian mystical poetry, and the one offering the lover can make, as he lies prostrate at the threshold of the friend, is his heart's blood, betokened by the bitter tears he sheds. Thus Ḥāfiẓ speaks of himself as '*Gharib u 'āshiq u bidil . . .*'—'Forlorn lover, seeking his lost heart in poverty and bewilderment.' So, too, the journey to the beloved is described, not merely as a stony and thorny road in the midst of the desert, but as a dangerous voyage through a stormy sea. Thus in the first ode of his *Divān* (first, of course, simply because the rhyme is in alif), Ḥāfiẓ has the line:

> Dark is the night, fearsome the waves, cruel the whirlpool:
> How should the light-hearted travellers on the shore know ought of how it fares with us?

No wonder, then, that the traveller on the spiritual Way is called upon to choose a sure guide and to keep a stout heart!

If, throughout the 'stages', we have found that, although by definition they are the results of human effort (*mujāhada*), they are neverthelss interpreted constantly by the Ṣūfi teachers as fruits also of grace and of supernatural surrender to its instigations, the penetration of a mystical spirit becomes far more noticeable in the case of the last two stages, *tawakkul* and *riḍā*.

6. 'TAWAKKUL'—TRUST OR SELF-SURRENDER

Tawakkul is the attitude of one who entrusts himself and all his ways and works to God, in a spirit of complete and unreserved trust. This is an attitude which springs naturally from the fundamental Islamic position. 'Islām' itself means self-surrender to God and the Muslim is he who has, once and for all, performed this act of submission and surrender. The religion of Islam is deeply marked with the sense of God's transcendance and man's insignificance and impotence. There has always been a tendency for Muslims who take their religion very much in earnest and *au pied de la lettre*, to push this principle of utter dependence on God to a point where the efficacity of human effort seems to be called in question, and the use of *asbāb* (secondary causes) invalidated. As mystics are among those who take their religion very much in earnest, it was only natural that, among the early Ṣūfis, many were found who seemed to push the principle of human reliance on God alone to an imprudent degree. It will be seen later on how mystics such as Maulānā Rūmi, with their supernatural gift of common sense, reacted effectively against such exaggerations.

In any case, *tawakkul* (self-surrender), in its precise position on the mystic path, reveals itself as vitally linked with the *ahwāl* which are manifestations of grace. More and more, as we approach the last of the preparatory stages of the Way, the mounting current of grace tends to take charge and to swing us past our carefully charted buoys and moorings. The very word for grace most commonly used by Muslim theologians is *faiḍ*, which expresses an overflow of beneficence.

Tawakkul, say the Ṣūfi theologians, has its root and efficient cause in *tawḥid,* that is, in profound belief in the divine unity —under which term they have in mind that which, in the divine Being, gathers up the threads of all beings and doings. The great Ṣūfi theologian, Ghazāli (Algazel, as he was known to the medieval scholastics) has, in the fourth Part of his *Iḥyā 'ulūm ed-Din,* a chapter entitled *Tawḥid wa Tawakkul,* and he deals with the same subject in his Persian work, the *kimiyāyi sa'ādet* (secret of happiness).

In the *Iḥyā,* he says that those who belong to what he calls the 'pith or marrow' of *tawḥid* are those who live very close to God and who, by an inner illumination of the divine light, are convinced that all things, however numerous or varied, spring from one source. Those whom he calls the 'pith of the pith' are those whose identity is completely swallowed up in the divine unity (*fanā*).

However valuable these explanations may be, they show us clearly that Ghazāli here presupposes that the *mutawakkil* has already moved out of the sphere of unaided human striving into that of supernatural prevenience. If this teaching was made into a logical whole, it would have to admit a supernatural *ḥāl* alongside each of the *maqāmāt*—a *mawhiba* (gift) backing up each *mujāhada.*

The fact is, that, at this stage, as at every stage, the genuine traveller on the way of truth and perfection aims at losing sight of his own existence (*wujūd*) and at dispossessing himself of his achievements and acquisitions. We have an illustration of this in the story of how Hussein b. Manṣūr Ḥallāj seeing Ibrahim Khawwāṣ on a journey, asked him what he was about. 'I am travelling,' replied Ibrahim, 'in order to increase my trust in God and my well-being.'

Upon this Ḥallāj exclaimed: 'You spend your whole life in cultivating your own interior. Where, then, is this famous forgetfulness in the divine unity?'

Still more striking, perhaps, is the story of Bāyazid Bisṭāmi and the disciple of Shaqiq of Balkh. This disciple was setting out on the pilgrimage to Mecca. Shaqiq told him to begin by paying a visit to Bāyazid. The disciple duly paid his visit and was asked by the great man what manner of sheikh Shaqiq was. He replied with an enthusiastic eulogy of his *Pir*'s spirit of trust in God: even were the heavens to turn to brass for years and the earth to cease to germinate, Shaqiq's trust would never fail.

Bāyazid exclaimed that this was shocking. If Shaqiq had said such a thing, he was no better than a heretic and an infidel.

The disciple, horrified and scandalized, renounced his pilgrimage and hastened back to his master who, when he heard the cause of his alarm, sent him back to Bāyazid, telling him to ask how Bāyazid himself was, what was *his* spiritual position.

Bāyazid at first refused to answer. The disciple pressed him to give him some reply, preferably in writing, that he could take back to his master. Bāyazid then wrote: *Bismillāh irraḥmān irraḥim*[1]: that is Bāyazid'.

He made it plain in this way that a spiritual Master must be entirely lost (*fāni*) in the divine Unity. He has no personal description. He cannot be cabined and confined even by his own *tawakkul*.

However, it is often a humble matter like daily bread which provides a handy test of a person's trust.

Bāyazid Bisṭāmi once assisted at the ritual prayer on a Friday. At the close of it the prayer-leader (*imām*) entered into conversation with Bāyazid. He said: 'I can't understand what you live on. You do not work for wages and you never ask alms from anyone . . .'

On this Bāyazid cried: 'Wait! I must perform this prayer again! A prayer recited behind an imām who does not know who gives us our daily bread cannot be valid.'

It was related of Hāṭim Aṣamm that he once asked Aḥmad Ḥanbal, the famous jurist, if he sought for his daily bread. 'Of course I do,' replied Hanbal.—'When do you seek it, afterwards, beforehand or at the time?'

Hanbal reflected that, if he replied 'Beforehand', his

[1] 'In the Name of God the merciful, the clement'—the first words of the *Qorān*.

questioner would ask why he wasted his time so. If he replied 'Afterwards', he would be asked why he sought a thing he had already obtained. If he replied 'At the time', the question would be, why he sought for something which was on the point of being given him. So he was reduced to silence.

A great teacher remarked on this point that Ḥanbal ought to have written the following reply: 'Seeking my daily bread is neither an obligation nor a duty nor a custom recommended by the example of the fathers. Why seek for something for which, as the Prophet said, God Himself seeks on our behalf?'

Hāṭim's answer is: 'It is our business to worship Him as He bade us. It is His business to provide us with daily sustenance, as He promised us.'

Maulānā Rūmi, who 'saw life steadily and saw it whole' has broader views as to the wisdom and the limits of *tawakkul*. In the first book of the *Maṣnavi* he recounts a debate between the beasts of the chase and the lion as to the relative advantages of trust in God and self-exertion. One cannot but feel that the fervour with which the aforesaid beasts recommend the lion to practise trust in God arises in part from their fears as to the consequences were he to launch out in their regard into a campaign of unrestrained activity. Still, in the long run, it is in the mouth of the lion that Rūmi puts his most telling arguments in favour of exertion and free will.

When the beasts advise him to put aside precautions and put all his trust in God, the lion replies: 'Yes. But if trust in God is the true guide, use of the means too is the Prophet's rule (*sunna*). He said: Trust in God and tie your camel's leg. Remember (the tradition): The earner (*kāsib*) is beloved of God; through trusting in God, do not become neglectful of the ways and means (*asbāb*).'

The beasts return to their contention that it is better to resign oneself to God's decrees: often men flee from trouble only to fall into another trouble, they recoil from the snake only to encounter the dragon. They go on: 'Since our sight is so defective, go, let your own sight pass away (*fanā*) in the sight of the friend. His sight in place of ours: what a bargain! In His sight you will find the whole object of your desire. He who gives rain from heaven is also able, from His mercy, to give us bread.'

'Yes,' said the lion, 'but the Lord has set a ladder before the feet of His servants. Step by step must we climb towards the roof; to be a necessitarian here is to indulge in foolish hopes. You have feet: why do you make yourself out to be lame? When the master put a spade in the slave's hands, he understood, without a word, what his intention was. Hand and spade alike are signs of His purpose. Our power of reflecting on the end is equivalent to an encouragement from Him. When you take His signs to heart, you will devote your life to fulfilling His implied desires. Then He will give you many hints as to mysteries. If you take up His burden, He will bear you aloft. If you accept His command, you will become the spokesman thereof; if you seek union with Him, thereafter you will be raised to union. To exercise freewill is, in effect, to thank God for His beneficence. Your necessitarianism is the denial of that beneficence.

'Thanksgiving for the power of acting freely increases your power; necessitarianism takes the gift out of your hand. . . . If you are putting trust in God, trust Him with your *work*: sow the seed, then rely upon the Almighty.'

The beasts, in reply to this, reminded their opponent how little trust can be reposed in human plans and doings, they 'gang aft agley'. And rightly so, since they are usually prompted by covetousness or ambition. In any case, if human activities aim at escaping from divine providence, they are doomed to disappointment.

'Yes,' said the lion, 'but remember also the exertions of the prophets and the true believers. God prospered their doings and sufferings: everything done by a good man is good. Their snares caught the heavenly bird, even their shortcomings turned to gain. Endeavour is not a struggle with destiny, because destiny itself has laid this task upon us.

'It is true that plans for making worldly gains are worthless, but plans for renouncing this world are divinely inspired. If a prisoner digs a hole in his prison, so as to escape, that is a good plot. If he plans to block it up, that is a foolish plot!

'The sceptic, in his very act of denying freewill, exercises it and proves it.'

After these conclusive arguments, the other beasts are silent.

7. 'RIḌĀ' (CONTENTMENT)

The last of the stages, following logically from *tawakkul* (submission), is *riḍā*. This denotes a condition in which the spiritual traveller is always pleased with whatever providence sends his way. *Riḍā* is akin to the Hebrew *ratsā*, the verbal noun derived from which is frequently met with in the Psalms and is usually translated by the Latin *beneplacitum*, or 'good pleasure'. It consists in a willing acceptance of whatever God sends, so that 'every wrinkle is smoothed away from the wayfarer's brow', since he is intimately convinced that 'on the path, whatever befalls the traveller is a blessing for him'. This condition of the wayfarer is attributed to his being the object of God's good pleasure and is a sign of it. It is easy to see, therefore, that this stage on the Way comes very close to a mystical state or gift of divine grace. In fact, in the third century of the Hijra, the mystical school which followed al-Muḥāsibi, most of whose members belonged to Khorasan, held that *riḍā*, a state of mutual satisfaction between God and the soul, was a *ḥāl*, or infused mystical state, a gift and not an acquisition. One who is in a 'stage' (*maqām*) is conscious of his own activity, whereas in the mystical state or *ḥāl*, self-consciousness disappears.

The School of Irāq, on the other hand, held *riḍā* to be a *maqām*.

Hujviri, in his *Kashf-ul-Maḥjūb* declares that *riḍā* begins as a *maqām* and ends as a *ḥāl*: it is, in fact, the pivot or turning point between the 'stages' and the 'states'.

This state of quiet contentment with God and all His ways, when the soul, convinced that destiny (*Qismet*) is never at fault, and that 'the Creator's pen never slipped', is always happy and well-pleased, is the fruit of perfect love of God. In it, the wayfarer will never open his mouth to make a request for destiny to be averted. If he makes petitions at all, it is solely in order to conform with the Lord's wish, expressed in the Scriptures: 'Ask of me and I will grant you your desires'.[1] So too, he regards always the present moment, not the past or the future. His cheerful and optimistic outlook, his freedom from all envy and avarice, his fervour and his liberty of heart spring from the same source.

In the third book of the *Maṣnavi*, Rūmi has a passage for which he himself provides a title:

> 'Description of some saints who are content with the divine ordinances and do not pray and beseech God to change this or that decree.'

'Now listen to a story of those travellers on the Way who have no objection in the world.' (The notion of an 'objection' is taken from the language of scholastic disputations.)

> 'Their mouths are closed to invocation. As they are possessed by a spirit of utter contentment and abandon, it has become unlawful for them to seek to avert destiny. God has revealed to their hearts such a good opinion of Him that they never don the dark blue garb (of mourning).'

Immediately after this passage, Rūmi illustrates the spirit and the outlook of the *ahl-i-riḍā'* (those who are always satisfied with God) by means of a dialogue between 'Buhlūl and a certain dervish':

> 'Buhlūl said to a certain dervish, "How art thou, O dervish?"
>
> 'The dervish replied, "How should that one be, according to whose desire the whole cosmic process goes on?—
>
> ' "According to whose desire the rivers and the torrents flow and the stars hold on their courses . . .," adding much more.
>
> 'Buhlūl tells him he has spoken truly: that is manifest in his spiritual radiance and glorious aspect. But he begs him to add some explanation of the mystery, so that it may come within the range of all, learned and unlearned.
>
> 'The dervish replies that it must be clear to all that "in

[1] *Qorān*, s. 40, v. 62.

all the earths and heavens not an atom moves a wing, not a straw turns, save by God's eternal and effectual command. When, therefore, His predestination becomes the pleasure of His servant, he becomes a willing slave to His decree. He no longer desires his life for himself, he lives for God's sake, not for riches; he dies for God's sake, not from fear or pain. . . . The servant of God who is thus disposed—does not the world move according to his command and behest?"'

FIVE

THE MYSTICAL STATES

As we have seen, the *maqāmāt* are the stages through which the wayfarer must pass in his strivings after perfection and in his efforts to dispose himself for the flooding in of mystical graces. Being moral and spiritual purifications and rectifications which can and must be brought about by the disciple's own efforts, they are known as 'acquired' (*iktisābi*) and not 'infused', the nearest word to which is, perhaps, *ladunni*. We come now to the *aḥwāl* (pl. of *ḥāl*), which, according to the customary Ṣūfi interpretation, represent mystical graces, sheer gifts of divine grace and generosity to a soul stripped of all self-seeking and self-regard. Henceforth, it is not so much the earnest striving and pressing forward of the pilgrim himself that is in the foreground, as the victorious and irresistible attraction of the divine beloved (*Jānān*), sweeping the traveller off his feet and carrying him along in a state of utter bewilderment.

The word *ḥāl* is not easy to translate. Like a number of other Ṣūfi terms, its meaning is not necessarily that which would be given in a dictionary. It is used in much subtler ways, which can be learnt only by familiarity with their writings. By its derivation it implies change, a changing state of soul. The *qalb* (heart) in which these mystic changes take place, is also, by definition, a changing thing, constantly turned this way and that by its divine transformer (*muqallib*). Hence it could almost be translated by 'phase' or 'mood'.

Jurjāni, in his *Book of Definitions,* defines it thus:
'The dictionary meaning of *ḥāl* is the end of the past and the beginning of the future (in other words, it is the present moment). But among the people of God (i.e. the Ṣūfis), it is an

experience of the soul (or heart), not artificially produced, not induced or acquired, of joy or sorrow, contraction or expansion, and so on. It passes away on the emergence of the attributes of the self. If it lasts and becomes a habitus, or fixed quality, it is called a *maqām*.[1]

Jurjāni here uses the word *maqām*, not as a transient stage but as a permanent mystical state. There was a marked diversion of opinion among the Ṣūfi teachers, as to whether a *ḥāl* could ever be permanent. According to the great teacher Junayd of Baghdād, who is followed in general by the School of Irāq, the *aḥwāl* are essentially transitory. 'The states (*aḥwāl*),' he says, 'are like flashes of lightning. If they last, that must be attributed to a psychical abnormality.' In another passage, where Junayd seems to derive the word *ḥāl* from the root *ḥalla*, to come down, he says: 'The states (*aḥwāl*) resemble what the word itself implies: they come down into the heart and disappear again.'

Abunasr Sarrāj, in his *Kitāb ul Luma'* distinguishes the following ten mystical phases or graces:

1. *Murāqaba* (literally, watching or observation, in this case, of one's own inner consciousness).
2. *Qurb* (or realization of the nearness of God).
3. *Maḥabba* (or love).
4. Fear (filial) and 5. Hope.
6. *Shauq* (longing, yearning).
7. *Uns* (a state of loving familiarity with God).
8. *Iṭminān* (a sense of security and serene dependence).
9. Contemplation (*Mushāhada*).
10. *Yaqin* (certainty).

It must be admitted at once that, in the case of several, at least, of these *aḥwāl*, the element of supernatural passivity is scarcely to be traced directly. Indirectly, of course, the influence of grace, its attraction (*kashish* or *jaẓba*), is always liable to make itself felt, even in the *maqāmāt*.

[1] *Ta'rifāt*, Cairo edition, p. 36.

I. 'MURAQABA' (WATCHING)

Murāqaba is defined by Jurjāni as 'the servant of God's constant realization of the Lord's awareness of all his states'.

The Ṣūfi authors refer us to the traditional saying of the Prophet: 'Worship God as if you saw Him. If you do not see Him, He, at any rate, sees you'.

Three categories are distinguished of the *ahl i murāqaba*—those who find themselves in this 'state':

(a) Those who, because of this knowledge of God's presence and awareness, instinctively ward off all evil thoughts.

(b) Those who are so intensely aware of His presence that they become oblivious to all created things.

As an illustration of this state, a story is related of Shibli. He went to see the well-known mystic Nūri and found him in such an intense state of *murāqaba* that not a hair of his body moved. He asked him, 'From whom did you learn this deep concentration?'—'From a cat watching by a mouse's hole. But his concentration is much more intense than mine.'

A similar story is told of Khafif, who went a long distance to visit two well-known Ṣūfis. They were so absorbed that they did not return his greeting. Their example had such an influence on him that he remained with them three days, neither eating nor drinking. When he pleaded with them to give him some piece of advice before he left, one of them, at last, told him that their most potent advice was that contained in their example.

(c) Those who have abandoned themselves and their state, whatever it is, to God as their trustee and protector. These, then, forgoing the veil of selfhood, are alone with God alone.

Someone said to Junayd of Bāghdād, 'You say, do you not, that there are three veils (between the soul and God): self, folk and world (*nafs, khalq, dunyā*)'. He replied, 'These are the veils of the common folk. The veils of God's intimates are: the sight of their good deeds, the sight of their merits, the sight of their charism (*kerāma*)'. He meant that one must strive after a stage where one loses sight of one's own state of *murāqaba*, so entirely and utterly has it taken possession of one's whole being.

If, however, the mirror of the human heart is to reflect the 'forms of the Unseen', the aspirant after divine knowledge must never cease polishing his heart. In the fourth book of the *Maṣnavi*,[1] Maulānā Rūmi says:

'If thou wilt be observant and vigilant, thou wilt see at every moment the response to thy action. . . . Be observant if thou wouldst have a pure heart, for something is born to thee in consequence of every action. And if thou hast an aspiration greater than this, if the enterprise goes beyond the (spiritual rank of the) observant, then, though thou be dark-bodied like iron, make a practice of polishing, polishing, polishing, that thy breast may become a mirror full of images, with a lovely silver-breasted form reflected therein on every side. If the earthen body is gross and dark, polish it—for it is receptive to the polishing instrument—in order that the forms of the unseen may appear in it, and that the reflection of houri and angel may dart into it.

'God hath given thee the polishing instrument, reason, to the end that thereby the leaf (surface) of the heart may be made resplendent. Thou, O prayerless man, hast put the polisher in bonds and hast released the two hands of sensuality. If bonds be put on sensuality, the hand of the polisher will be untied. A piece of iron that became a mirror of the unseen—all the forms (of the unseen) would be shot into it. But thou hast darkened thy heart and let the rust into thy nature. Do it no more.'

2. QURB ('NEARNESS')

Qurb, the sense of God's nearness, is induced by practice of the state of *murāqaba* or concentration. The Ṣūfis often quote texts from the *Qorān* such as: 'If my worshippers ask thee about me, well, I am near' (Sura 2, verse 182);

'We are nearer to him than his own neck-vein' (Sura 50, v. 15); and 'We are nearer to Him than you, but you do not perceive' (Sura 56, verse 84).

Sarrāj says that this state consists in beholding one's nearness to God so that one seeks ever to draw nearer to Him by

[1] Prof. Nicholson's version.

means of good deeds and constant remembrance (*ẓikr*). He divides the 'people of nearness' (*ahl i qurb*) into three categories:

(1) Those whose efforts to draw nigh to Him are prompted by their knowledge that He is all-knowing, that He is close to them and dominates them. (Clearly, these are still in the realm of *mujāhada* and *kasb*, virtuous effort.)

(2) Those deep investigators who, whatever they see, see God nearer to it than they themselves.

(3) Men of ultimates (ultimate realizations, men who go the whole way). These are so completely lost (*fāni*) in Him that they are no longer conscious of their own state of nearness. (It is this third group that is touched by the mystical attraction.)

This *qurb*, this nearness to God, is not, says Rūmi, a nearness of time and place:

> 'To be nigh unto God is not to go up or down. To be nigh unto God is to escape from this prison of existence (i.e. self).
>
> 'What room hath non-existence for "up" and "down"? Non-existence hath no "soon" or "far" or "late". . . .
>
> 'The friends of God are so glad at the bottom of the pit that they are afraid of the throne and the tiara.
>
> 'Every place where the Beloved Himself is their companion is above the sky, not below the earth.'[1]

3. 'MAHABBA': THE 'HAL', OR MYSTICAL STATE, OF LOVE

Love, consummated in vision or in union, as it is the final goal of the wayfarer, is likewise the propelling and sustaining power of his life and journey. To that extent, all other stages are but preludes or consequences and effects of Love.

For the Ṣūfi God is the one beloved, the Jánán, the supremely beautiful and desirable object of the soul's passionate love, as it strives with unutterable longing to reach Him and lose itself in Him. In reality, it is the supreme beloved who draws the soul towards Himself with compulsive magnetism, whether by His own incomparable love or by His scarcely concealed beauty (*Jamál*).

[1] *Maṣnavi*, Book 3, verses 4510–4515.

Kuntu kanzan makhfian . . .', declares the Hadith, 'I was a hidden treasure and I yearned to be known. I created the world in order to be known'. Traces of Him, of His beauty and love, are thus to be found in every created being, not least in the human soul, in its loving nature and its attraction to beautiful things. Mingled with intense longing for Him and a sweet sense of being desired and called by Him is a piercing grief at being separated from Him (*firáq*) and a certain bewilderment (*taḥayyur*), almost despair, resembling that of the moth dashing itself to death against the flame, or the nightingale singing its heart out as it serenades the unattainable rose.

This is the supreme passion, arising from the supreme intuition. It is not the result of metaphysical reasoning.

On the other hand it is the source and motive of all renouncements, above all the renouncement of self (*wujúd*).

While the wayfarer gets a glimpse of the divine in human beauty and love, he can never stay there, he must always be passing beyond to the one who transcends time, place and measurement. But

'Whether it be of this world or of that,
'Thy love will lead thee yonder at the last.'

This mysterious love is rightly put among the mystical, infused states. It cannot be acquired at will. Its birth and growth are both the work of divine, prevenient grace. Bāyazid Bisṭāmi once said: 'I thought I loved Him but, on second thoughts, I saw that His love preceded mine.' In another passage of his we find: 'Lovers of God, whether asleep or awake, seek and are sought. Still, they are not concerned with their own seeking and loving but are lost in contemplation of the beloved, in rapt attention to Him. It is a crime in the lover to regard his love and it is an outrage on love to regard one's own seeking while one is face to face with the sought (*al Maṭlúb*).' So, he sings: 'His love came into my heart and drove out all else, so that it remained single, as He is single.' In a similar strain Rūmi has:

'Love came and gave up my soul to the beloved;
'The beloved now gives me life from her (or his) own life.'

And again:

'O heart, as you go to that Sweetheart you must lose your heart:
'Heedless go to the audience-chamber of Union.
'When you have reached His door, hidden from every creature,
'Leave yourself outside and then go in.'

Concerning such a one Rūmi sang:

'Love came and like blood filled my veins and tissues,
'Emptied me of myself and filled me with the Friend.
'The friend has taken possession of every atom of my being.
'The name is all that I have left now: all the rest is He.'

In an even earlier period Attar wrote these glowing words, which a devout client of the Sacred Heart need not repudiate:

'Fiercer than thine the fire within His breast,
'His Heart beats faster than that heart of thine.
'Stay within that burning Heart of His
'And thou'lt learn His Love is infinite.'

4. THE FEAR OF THE LORD

Fear, even when it is filial or reverential fear, plays but a minor rôle in the spiritual doctrine of the Ṣūfis. It enters far more into the lives and outlook of the early school of Semitic pietists who, in this, were certainly more in agreement with the dominant trend of the *Qorān* and the Moslem way of life. With the Ṣūfi or '*ārif* ('gnostic') of the third century of the Hijra onwards, speculation of a more intellectualist kind transforms the spiritual outlook and, above all, love, taking more and more to itself, 'casts out fear'. Fear is not considered as a perfection in itself: it is but the moderator of hope. The consummate mystic is independent of hope and fear alike. He is illumined as to the way, its stages and its end or goal. 'Light has dawned', as Mawlānā Jalālu' ddin Rūmi says, 'and the traveller has followed the sun.'

5. THE STATE OF HOPE

The Ṣūfi holds that to worship God in the hope of His grace and bounty is better than to worship Him in fear of punishment. But hope, as it exists in the heart of the adept, is based neither on his own merits nor even on his conviction of the infinite broadness of God's mercy. It is concerned with God Himself and Him alone:—hope in God—*rijā fillāh*—he asks from God nothing but Himself, caring nothing for paradise and the houris, the *fardāyi zāhid*—the devotee's tomorrow. Thus Sheikh Ansāri exclaims:

'O Lord, I, this beggar, seek from Thee something,
'Seek from Thee more than a thousand kings.
'Everyone comes to Thy door seeking something:
'Now I have come and what I seek from Thee is Thyself.

The sixth, seventh and eighth of the mystical states enumerated by Sarraj are *Shauq* (longing), *Uns* (loving familiarity) and *Itminan* (trust or confidence). As they are all fruits of loving resignation, there is nothing new we can say of them here.

9. 'MUSHAHADA' (CONTEMPLATION)

Although the ten mystical states are not necessarily arranged in progressive order of importance or sequence in time, it is not for nothing that the great themes of contemplation and *yaqin* (certainty) form the culmination of the series. It is true that Ṣūfi teaching is a practical training in the methods and requirements of perfection, but this perfection, the goal of all spiritual wayfarers, is conceived of by all Persian mystics as essentially a matter of knowledge: not the knowledge acquired by reading books and studying exercise-books, by disputation and reasoning, but that direct knowledge of God Himself which is bestowed on hearts rightly disposed and duly prepared by an act of sheer grace and bounty.

Thus the very same impulse which aimed at enlivening and interiorizing Islam strove, at the same time, to infuse into it a spirit of intelligence, of intellectual curiosity, of original investigation and speculation, summed up in the term *ijtihád*. In this effort the Persian spiritual intelligentsia were but renewing the rarely broken tradition of their country's ancient function in the world. That the Ṣūfis should have welded so wonderfully into a consistent whole the purest religious feeling with the most daring and uncompromising thought, and, in addition, clothed the result in some of the loveliest and most winning poetry that had ever been written, is but to say that, in their own age, they gave supreme expression to the genius of their race.

There is much evidence in the writings of the Persian mystics of the influence of the Neo-Platonists, whose teachings, including the so-called 'theology of Aristotle', were widely disseminated in the Near East and in Persia. In Syria, one of the most notable fruits of this Neo-Platonic fertilization on Christian soil was the writings of Denis the (pseudo-) Areopagite, which, owing to a misunderstanding as to their real origin, were treated with the utmost attention and veneration by Christian theologians and spiritual writers, including St Thomas Aquinas. Similar doctrines produced similarly startling effects in Persia and, before long, in countries newly won to the Islamic faith. There can be no doubt that the charm exercised by these doctrines, as also by Buddhist teaching, was among the chief causes of the Persian mystical movement in post-Islamic times.

In earlier chapters we have studied the different stages on the way to the mystical goal. These, however, are but means to an end, a form of training or preparation. The end is the contemplation of God, the vision of the divine beauty, unveiled. 'This borrowed life of mine, handed over to me by the friend,' cries Háfiẓ, 'I shall hand back to Him when at last I see His face.' All the Ṣūfi theologians are agreed in this, that the purpose of man's creation was that he should come to know God. Man is, we are told, the eye with which God surveys Himself. Or he is the mirror which God holds up to Himself. One of the traditions most often quoted by them is: *Kuntu kanzan makhfian* . . .—'I was a hidden treasure and I wanted to become known, so I created the world to make myself known.' The *shahâda* itself (*Lā ilāha illā 'llāh*)[1] illustrates this great movement of going forth and return (*min al mabda ila'l ma'ád*). The emanation of created things, things other (*ghair*) than God (*ma siwá'llāh*), is shown by the words *lā ilāha* (No God), while their return to Him is indicated by *illā'llāh* (but God). This is the consummation of *tawḥid* (unification), the re-integration of all things in the one from whom they sprang.

Man is the culmination of the movement out of God into the darkness of multiplicity. But he is also the beginning of the arc of return. He is the *maṭla' ul fajr*, the dawn of day, a day whose high noon-tide is to be unclouded glory.

This ultimate divine destiny set before man is the accomplishment of the original covenant (*mithāq*) made between God and man on the *rūz i alast*—the day of 'Am I not?' (your Lord). This *rūz i alast* refers to a passage (verse 171) in the Seventh sura of the *Qorān*, relating ostensibly to the Jews, but understood in a universal sense by the mystics: 'When thy Lord brought forth their descendants from the reins of the sons of Adam and took them to witness against themselves, "Am I not," said He, "your Lord?" They said, "Yes." ' The passage is interpreted by the Ṣūfi mystics as signifying a primal pact, entered into before Creation between God and His creatures, the latter being represented by the pre-existent form (*ṣūrat*) or archetypal idea of Adam, in which was prefigured the divine aspect of humanity (*nāsūt*). The reply *Baly* (Yea) is interpreted by orthodox Mohammedan theologians as an acknowledgment of God's right to judge men's actions and punish their sins. The Ṣūfis for their part laid stress rather on the love which here displayed itself and was responded to in the state of pre-existence. All human souls heard the divine question *a lastu bi rabbikum*? and answered *Baly*, but each one's confession had a different value according to his nature and disposition. The elect (*as-sābiqūn*), enlightened by love, replied: 'Yea; Thou art He whom we love and adore'. True believers (*asḥābu'l maymana*): 'Yea; Thou art the one Lord whom we worship'. Hypocrites and infidels, whose hearts were veiled by

[1] 'There is no god but God.'

the attributes of divine majesty and indignation, gave the response unwillingly, like slaves under duress.

Those happy souls, therefore, who enjoy mystical union in this life, are those who were destined to it on that day of *alast*. 'The spirit of him who, at the time of *alast*, saw his Lord and became beside himself and intoxicated with extatic love, that spirit knows the scent of the wine because he drank it before', says Maulānā Rūmi in the second book of the *Maṣnavi*. This doctrine evidently represents a form of anamnesis. 'Are there not signs, too, in your own selves?' asks the *Qorān*, and the mystical soul recognizes these signs, whether in the frequent incidence of suffering and affliction or in the interior attractions towards divine union which he experiences in himself.

10. 'YAQIN' (CERTITUDE)

In the enumeration found in the *Kitāb ul Luma* of Sarráj, the state of contemplation is followed by that of *yaqin* or certainty, the state of one who has become firmly rooted in divine contemplation and the process of *fanā* and *baqā*. It may be said, therefore, to be the term or goal of all the states or *aḥwāl*. In this state all doubt has vanished and 'joy over good news' takes its place. *Yaqin*, indeed, is not only the culmination, but the pith and marrow of all the mystical states. It is defined by Jurjāni (*Ta'rifāt*) as 'clear vision through the power of faith, not by proof or demonstration'. Even within this state one can advance from *'ain al yaqin* (the essence of certainty) to *haqq al yaqin* (the reality of certainty). This is a development of a passage in the *Qorān*, sura 102, 'The desire to surpass one another in wealth distracts you. Nay, if ye but knew with the knowledge of certainty (*'ilm al yaqin*)! Verily ye shall see Hell-fire. I say again, Verily ye shall see it with the vision of certainty ([1]*ayn al yaqin*)'. The passage is quoted by Rūmi in the third book of the *Maṣnavi*, verse 4122. In connection with it, he says:

'Know that knowledge is a seeker of certainty, and certainty is a seeker of vision and intuition.

'Seek this now in (the Sūra beginning) *Alhākum* . . .

'Knowledge leads to vision, O knowing one: if it became certainty, they would see Hell.

'Vision is immediately born of certainty, just as fancy is born of opinion.

'See in *Alhākum* the explanation of this, that the knowledge of certainty becomes the intuition of certainty.

'I am higher than opinion and certainty, and my head is not to be turned aside by blame.

'Since my mouth ate of His sweetmeat, I have become clear-eyed and a seer of Him.'

SIX

HOMESICKNESS (Firáq)

FOR the pilgrim, this life is a time of separation from the beloved. He sighs perpetually after reunion with his eternal friend. His complaint, in effect, in Rūmi's words, is:

'*Murgh i bāgh i malakūtam, nayam az 'ālam i khāk . . .*'—
'I am a bird of God's garden, I do not belong to this dusty world.
'For a day or two they have locked me up in the cage of my body.
'I did not come here of myself, how should I return of myself?
'He who brought me must take me back again to my own country.'

The poet reverts to this theme when he sings:

'That imprisoned nightingale called the soul—
'Has no power in himself to break open the cage.
'On that day when, at last, this business of reunion is brought off,
'And this bird flies off from its cage,
'My spirit, having heard the King calling, Come back! (*irja'i!*),
'In one great flight, will go back to the King's hand.'

The call of the King from the invisible world lifts the soul away from all care for the affairs of this world:

'You must know that whoever hears God's call
'Lays aside all care for the business of this world.
'Whoever has to do with God on high

'Is received in audience Yonder and gives up work here Below.' (Rūmi.)
(There is a play here on the words *kār u bār*.)

It is, however, in the Poem to the *Maṣnavi* that Jalālu' ddin Rūmi gives finest expression to the yearning of the soul for reunion with the One from whom it has been torn: indeed, the poet seems to hint that this 'wailing of the reed' sums up the whole message of the *Maṣnavi* itself.

'Listen to the reed how it tells a tale, complaining of separations,
'Saying, "Ever since I was parted from the reed-bed, my lament has caused man and woman to moan.
'It is only to a bosom torn by severance that I can unfold the pain of love-desire.
'Everyone who is left far from his source wishes back the time when he was united with it.
'In every company I uttered my wailful notes, I consorted with the unhappy and with them that rejoice.
'Everyone became my friend in his own opinion; none sought out my secrets from within me.
'My secret is not far from my plaint, but ear and eye lack the light (whereby it can be apprehended).
'Body is not veiled from soul, nor soul from body, yet none can see the soul.
'The wind that sounds in the reed is not wind but fire: whoso hath not this fire, may he be naught!
' 'Tis the fire of Love that is in the reed, 'tis the fervour of Love that is in the wine. . . .
'The reed tells of the Way full of blood and recounts stories of the passion of Majnūn." '

The lament of the reed, torn from its reed-bed, the soul's yearning for reunion with its divine source, the griefs and glooms of this vale of severance set the heart in a state of turmoil and bewilderment. Nothing created can satisfy it. On the other hand, the divine beloved seems so sublime, so dissimilar, that a human heart's love for Him appears to resemble that of the nightingale for the rose, or that of the moth for the candle. The pilgrim on the blood-stained path stumbles along, 'poor, heart-sick, forlorn and bewildered'. He has 'suffered the trials of fortune and the weals and bruises of separation'. But still he is urged on by his ceaseless longing, drawn along, if the truth were known, by the irresistible attraction of the eternal beauty. Dimly, but with supernatural certainty, he knows that the sight of God is the one thing that can satisfy the infinite yearnings of his finite heart. And where is he to look for Him? He might wander round the whole world in vain. *Yār dar khāneh*—'The friend is in our own home all the time'. In order to know our Lord, we must first learn to know ourselves. *Man 'arafa nafsahu, 'arafa Rabbahu* is a traditional proverb which is often on the lips or the pen of the mystic. The pilgrim on the way to the presence must lay aside veil after veil of his carnal notions and desires, must put aside all desire 'of this world and the next', and come to rest in the pure, unadulterated ground of his being, the 'heart' or the 'secret' (*Sirr* or *khafi*). It is here that the divine image—or should we say, the divine being Himself?—is to be found. As was to be expected, Islām has not let itself be deprived of a 'tradition', to the effect that God made man *'ala ṣūratihi,* in His image. Constantly, man must seek to discover in himself the divine likeness. In the book *Fihi mā fihi,* Jalālu'ddin Rūmi says: 'Man is the astrolabe of God, but it needs an astronomer to understand the astrolabe. "He that knows himself, knows his Lord." Just as, by means of an astrolabe, the astronomer observes the revolutions and discovers the state of the heavenly bodies, so when man has received from God the gift of self-knowledge by means of the astrolabe of his being, which is a divine mirror, he continually beholds the manifestation of the divine beauty, without attributes and beyond description; and of that beauty this mirror is never void.'

To say that God created man in His image is, therefore, to say that He created in man, as the very root and spiritual core of his nature, the heart (*dil* or *qalb*) and soul (*jān, rūh,* or, sometimes, *nafs-i-nāṭiqah*). It is true that man has also been furnished with reason (*'aql*) or understanding, but its functions are limited to the sphere of created things and it cannot rise to knowledge of God Himself. 'Heart' and 'soul', together with expressions like *sirr* and *khafi*, signify, at bottom, the same reality, but 'heart' (*dil* or *qalb*) is almost invariably used where mystical knowledge is in question and *sirr* and *khafi* (secret) are used to reinforce the sense of an organ exclusively ordered to divine contemplation. The 'heart' is capable of knowing the divine essence itself and, therefore, the true inwardness of all things. When lit up by the light of faith, it becomes the mirror in which all divine knowledge is manifested. According to a saying attributed to Mahomet, speaking on behalf of God: 'My earth and my heaven cannot contain me but the heart of my believing servant contains me.'

The state of purity and clarity needed for this mirroring is, however, in practice, rarely attained. Too often, the heart is veiled and obscured by negligence and inattention, and material and sensual images soil and darken it.

The heart, though capable of such heights of knowledge, is still a human organ. It is disputed ground between the opposing forces of God and wisdom on the one hand and the devil and evil passions on the other. Each side tries to invade it. By one channel divine knowledge enters it, by another, the whisperings of sensuality.

> 'A strange composition indeed is man, made up of angel and beast;
> 'If he inclines to this, he falls lower than this, if he inclines to that, he improves on that.'

As a human organ, moreover, the heart is the living link between the spirit (*rūḥ*) and the animal soul (*nafs*): it receives the effusions of the spirit and, in its turn, exerts an influence on the sphere of the senses and feelings.

Its name in Arabic, *qalb*, often used by the Persians, is referred to the root *qalaba*, meaning to turn or turn over. We are told that this word well befits the heart, since it is constantly rotating or turning from divine manifestations to created phenomena and vice versa.

To keep the mirror of the heart in a high state of polish is the spiritual man's constant preoccupation, although, in the last resort, its perfect polish and freedom from rust and dust is a gift of grace (*tawfiq*). (The mirrors referred to by these early mystics were, of course, made of steel.) The chief film on the inner mirror is the film of self. Says Rūmi (*Maṣnavi*, Bk. I):

> 'Like polished iron, lose the ferruginous colour; become in thy ascetical discipline like a mirror without rust.
> 'Make thyself pure from the attributes of selfhood, that thou mayst behold thy own pure, untarnished essence,
> 'And behold within thy heart all the sciences of the prophets, without book and without preceptor and master.'

Rūmi then proceeds: 'If you desire a parable of the hidden knowledge, I will relate the story of the Greeks (*Rūmiyyān*) and the Chinese.' This story had been related by Ghazāli, in a slightly different form, in his *Ihyā* (III, 22, 18). A king, desiring to have his palace decorated, called in a group of Chinese artists and another of Anatolians. Each side claimed superiority in their art. The king, to test them, gave them two rooms facing each other. A curtain was drawn across the entrance. The Chinese called for a great variety of paints. The Anatolians said they would do nothing but remove rust. Both sides set to work, the Chinese painting, painting, the Anatolians burnishing away. When the Chinese had finished, filled with joy and pride, they called the king in to see their work. He was ravished at the sight. Then he visited the Anatolians. They drew the curtain aside and the Chinese painting, reflected on the burnished wall, seemed now transformed into something far more beautiful.

The Anatolians, Rūmi then says, are the Ṣūfis. They are independent of study, books and erudition, but they have burnished their breasts and made them pure from greed and avarice and hatred. The purity of the mirror is, beyond doubt, the heart which receives images innumerable. The mirror of the heart hath no bound. Here the understanding is reduced to silence, or else it leads into error, because the heart is with Him, or indeed the heart is HE. They that burnish their hearts have escaped from scent and colour; they behold beauty at every moment without tarrying. They have relinquished the outer form and husk of knowledge, they have raised the banner of the essence of certainty. Thought is gone and they have gained light; they have gained the land and sea of gnosis. They receive a hundred impressions from the empyrean and the starry sphere and the void: what do I say, impressions? Nay, 'tis the very sight of God.'

There is, moreover, in the sixth book of the *Maṣnavi*, a passage in which Rūmi says that the perfect man is 'God Himself in the likeness of a reflection'.

In this connection, one of Rūmi's commentators quotes the following lines from Jāmi:

> 'If one regards only the state of the *mirror*, it is impossible for him to see the *image*;
> 'And he whose eye is fixed on the image will find that the mirror has vanished in the image.
> 'When the divine mystery is revealed to the soul, there rises from it the cry "Glory unto Me (*subḥāni*)!" '

Persian poets designate this God-revealing mirror of the human heart by the term *jām i Jam*, or 'Jamshid's mirror (or cup)'. This legendary mirror, perhaps thought of as a crystal globe, is thus associated with the mythical Shāh of old Irān, Jamshid, the fourth king of the world in the ancient Persian epic. Jamshid, according to the *Avesta* (Vend. II) invented many arts and was honoured with frequent colloquies with God. When he succumbed to the temptation of pride and claimed to be an object of worship, he lost the aureole of majesty (*farr i izadi*) and had to yield the kingdom to the Arab Ḍahāk.

The name of Jamshid was subsequently attached to Solomon or to Alexander the Great and the world-revealing mirror (*jām i jahān-numā*) was said to have been erected for him at Alexandria by Aristotle.

Poets and mystics, however, always mean by the term the secret spiritual instrument or organ of universal knowledge, which, like some Iranian Grail, dominated their imagination.

Khoja Ḥāfiẓ of Shirāz wrote an ode in this connection which has become famous. It begins: *Sālhā dil ṭalab i jām i Jam az mā mikard* and, translated, runs as follows:

'For years our heart has been seeking Jamshid's glass of us,
'Begging from strangers what it already owned;
'Seeking from lost men on the sea-shore
'The pearl that is outside the confines of place and being.
'I took my difficulty to the Magian priest yesterday,
'So that, with his firm discernment, he might solve the riddle.
'I found him joyful and smiling, a goblet of wine in his hand,
'And in that mirror he was beholding a hundred sights.
'He whose heart, like a rose-bud, hid the secret of Reality,
'Noted the page of his mind from that copy.
'I asked him: When did the sage give you this world-surveying mirror?
'He answered: On that day when He created the blue vault of heaven.
'This forlorn man—God is with him at every turn, but he has not seen him and, as from afar, cries: My God, my God!
'That dear Comrade, said he, on whose account even the gibbet raised its head,
'His crime consisted in manifesting secret things.
'If the grace of the Holy Spirit vouchsafe help again,
'Others too may do what the Christ did.
'I said to him: What means the chain of the tresses of fair idols?
'He replied: Ḥāfiz is complaining of the length of Christmas night!'

As Ḥāfiz deliberately chose, in this poem, an enigmatic form of speech, I venture to add here some explanatory notes.

The 'Magian priest' (*Pir 'i mughān*), in such passages, stands either for a Magian or a Christian priest, or even for a tavern-keeper, whose chief recommendation, for the Ṣūfi, lay in the fact that, outside or in contravention of the Moslem law, such as he freely drank and dispensed wine, often choosing for the purpose solitary ruins (*kharābāt*) outside the town. Wine, for the Ṣūfi, stood for the joys of divine ecstasy and self-forgetfulness, proscribed by the narrow-minded Moslem moralists and theologians. What the Magian, therefore, held in the cup of his burnished heart was the wine of divine inspiration and ecstasy, in consequence of which, released from the trammels of self, he was able to contemplate the mysteries of both worlds.

The 'dear Comrade' is Manṣūr al Ḥallāj, with his famous *shatḥiyya* of *Anā'l ḥaqq* (I am God), for which apparent blasphemy he suffered death on a cross. In the next verse it seems to be suggested that grace might unite souls to the Christ in such a way that they participated, not only in His states but in His miraculous achievements. This, too, is clearly brought in as a supreme example of self-denial and God-consciousness.

The 'dark tresses of the idols' stand for created beauties and diversities which at once veil and reveal the identity of the hidden, divine Creator. These darknesses temper the radiance of the divine manifestation, just as the mid-winter darkness of Christmas night cloaks the glory of the heavenly King's appearance on earth.

Often the term *shab i yaldā* is misunderstood. *Yaldā* is the Chaldean word for the Nativity and was accordingly the word for Christmas with which Persians were familiar. Dictionaries now usually explain it as 'the darkest night of winter'.

The function of the 'heart' (*dil*) is, then, to mirror or reflect God and, in Him and through Him, the whole of creation. The steel mirror does not understand or love the object reflected in it. It is not *rázdár*, as Rūmi puts it, not a real sharer in the secret which it unwittingly reveals, whereas the heart of man is alive, aware, conscious, Godlike. If you would see God, then, look into the mirror of your heart, and look in such a way as to forget the mirror through absorption in the object it reflects and presents. In other words, the contemplation of God is not reflection on an idea evolved from the human mind. It is a gift of grace, granted to a heart that turns itself inwards to seek Him and await His revelation.

The interior experiences which accompany and bear witness

to this divine work in and on the soul are known under names such as *ḥāl, shirb, jazba, fanā*, all of which contain the sense of a delightful yielding to, or passing away into the influx of the divinity, a happy oblivion of self, a willing self-surrender to the adorable Invader. The mystic wayfarer, having yielded to this divine attraction (*jazba*), becomes *fāni* in God, disappears in Him.

SEVEN

LOST IN GOD (Faná)

THE term *fanà* expresses a notion which is fundamental in Persian mysticism. It may owe its origin to Indian sources, but the Persians themselves are responsible for the subtle and enlightening interpretations of *faná* which abound in their spiritual writings.

In the West eyebrows have often been raised over *faná* (compare, for instance, Fitzgerald's 'one moment in annihilation's waste', where, no doubt, 'annihilation' represents the author's understanding of the word *faná*.) It is natural for right-minded men to shudder and protest at the idea of annihilation. But there are no protests or shudderings when Walter Hilton or other Catholic mystics call for the personality to be 'noughted', or urge its 'breakdown', although the idea behind both terms would seem to be the same. We may go further and suggest that when Our Lord called upon His followers to 'lose themselves', or 'deny themselves', He was hinting at the same thing.

The Arabic word *fanā*, as a verb, means to disappear, vanish or perish, pass away. The Ṣūfi notion of *fanā*, therefore, seems to be that the transient, evanescent side of a man must 'pass away', in order that something or someone lasting may reign supreme in him. 'My breast is so full of thought of the beloved', sings Ḥāfiẓ, 'that the thought of self has disappeared from my consciousness'. In another passage of his *Divan* he has:

'Between the lover and the beloved there must be no veil;
'Thou thyself art thy own veil, Ḥāfiẓ—get out of the way!'

When God is realized to be all, there must and can no longer be any mention of 'me and thee'. Someone knocked and called out 'Who is there?' The Disciple, who had at first replied 'It is I', becoming wiser, now replied: 'Thyself!' And the Ṣūfi thesis is that it is the divine being himself who speaks through the mouth of Mansúr al Halláj when, in his ecstasy of God-consciousness and self-forgetfulness, he cries: *Anā'l Ḥaqq* (I am God). To advert to self would, for such a one, be a form of *shĭrk* or polytheism, a denial of the fundamental dogma: There is no god but God.

The suppression, by-passing or transcendance of human notions, fancies, desires, idiosyncrasies, is only the external and superficial aspect of this divine transformation. Above all, it is one's own self that has to be forgotten, renounced, out-passed. Yet this supreme experience can only be brought about by the Lord Himself, by an act of grace abounding, submerging all conscious traces of the individual self. This does not mean the elimination or destruction of the human personality. Indeed, the human personality *must* survive if it is to keep up this never-ending act of adoration and self-transcendance. It survives, one might say, rather as hydrogen or oxygen survive in water, by a sort of virtual substantiality. Henceforth, the life of the self is to live in and for another, in a sort of perpetual ecstasy or inebriation. This is supreme liberation and exultation. All else is forgotten, so wonderful is the sight that dawns on awakened eyes.

True, while this life lasts, a state of soberness (*ṣaḥw*), when consciousness of self returns, is bound to follow upon the stage of inebriation (*sukr*), when one had been gloriously lost to self. But as the refining process proceeds, the rhythm is speeded up. Bewilderment (*taḥayyur*) and the sense of estrangement from the world of limits and multiplicity increase. In the perfection of *fanā*, *fanā* itself is no longer adverted to: it is the state of *fanā ul fanā*, the disappearance of disappearance. The soul, going all out to God, no longer has any return upon itself. Very often, but not necessarily always, this state of absorption in God is accompanied by complete abstraction from the sense-world and utter obliviousness to time and place.

So great were the benefits, so wonderful the bliss of this state of abstraction from self, that some of the Ṣūfis, in their search for it, resorted to practices deliberately aimed at inducing the state of trance. This was, of course, a misguided deviation, witnessing to a confusion of values, a failure to appreciate the autonomy and prevenience of divine grace, as well as its transcendance of every merely physical phenomenon. If the effects of grace can be induced by artificial means, it is no longer grace but a form of man-made magic. Better the harsh winds of 'sobriety' than the soft Lydian airs of such self-induced trances and exaltations. The greatest Persian mystics are, indeed, at one with our own mystical teachers in holding that the real test of the genuineness of a mystical experience is to be found in its effects on the soul, the character: when there has been union with God, the soul will be filled with light and benevolence, it will long to pour out its treasures of knowledge and love upon hungry and thirsty souls.

There is another sense in which the doctrine of *fanā* is connected with the Ṣūfi theory of divine contemplation and union. The Ṣūfi masters took over from Aristotle the position that knowledge of an object demands a sort of proportion or adjustment in the knowing faculty and that the knowledge of which anyone is capable is measured by the conditions of his being. Hence, they concluded, if a man is to become capable of knowing God, of attaining to *ma'rifat* or gnosis, he must be divested of his merely human, created limitations, he must be lost to his finite self. Only when the divine being has filled the room left by a self-denying and self-surrendering human can such a one arrive at true knowledge of Him.

Psychologically speaking, moreover, it is the experience of mystics in every clime that with the advent of a supernatural influx comes an increasing or total suspension of the multiple and discursive activities of the mind. The intervention of grace has the effect of putting purely natural functioning out of action—or, perhaps, it is nearer the truth to say that the natural function is heightened to operate on a higher plane.

Notable evidence of this is to be found in the fact that those who have received a high mystical grace are reduced to silence. The wonder of the experience defeats and silences all human utterance. Thus the great mystic Junayd, of Baghdad, declared: 'When a man comes to know God, his tongue is silent'. And

Muḥammad ibn Wāsi': 'As for him who learns to know God, his speech grows rare and his bewilderment grows greater.'

In this state of affairs the disciple does not remain utterly inactive. He still has to do his part by detaching his heart from created things. And yet, even here, when God sets His heart on a man, He Himself sets out to detach that man in an efficacious way all His own.

The more the heart and mind are purged of *ghair* (aught else) the more strongly does a man feel the pull or attraction of the divine beloved, the *Jānān*.

It is then that the truth of Maghribi's Ode is realized, to wit, that

> 'By his own powers no one can find the way that leads to Him;
> 'Whoever walks towards Him walks with *His* foot.
> 'Until the beam of His love shines out to guide the soul,
> 'It does not set out to behold the love of His Face.
> 'My heart feels not the slightest attraction towards Him
> 'Until an attraction comes from Him and works upon my heart.
> 'Since I learnt that He longs for me, longing for Him never leaves me for an instant.
> 'So often has He set Himself opposite my sensitive heart that it has taken on His very ways and temperament.'

It is this divine attraction, therefore, and not any human effort as such, that effectively leads the soul to beatitude and salvation. Grace is subject to no human laws or conditions. Hence, as the Ṣūfi doctors point out, the study of the mystical life is completely different from disciplines such as physics or mathematics. Rūmi, in the first book of the *Maṣnavi*, in a passage where he comments on the Qorānic verse: 'What God wills happens, what He does not will does not happen,' declares:

> 'In the last resort
> 'Without the grace of God we are nought, nought.

'Without the favours of God and of His familiars
'Even an angel's page is smudged.'

When Sheikh Abū Said Abūl Khair was asked: 'When is the servant of God delivered from his debts?', he replied: 'When his Lord releases him. To attribute spiritual deliverance to one's own efforts and not to sheer grace (*tawfiq*) is idolatry or polytheism.' In this state, says Abū Said Kharrāz, if anyone asks you: 'Where are you from? And what do you want?', the only answer you can make to both questions is 'God'.

So, too, Shibli says that the Ṣūfi life is 'the disappearance of the merely human and the appearance of the sheer divine'.

Sheikh 'Aṭṭār, in the *Mantiq utṬair*, tells the wayfarer:

'Be noughted, so that thy being may come to thee from Him. While thou art, how can true being come to thee? Until thou art lost in lowliness and *fanā* (noughting), how will affirmation and permanence reach thee from the Almighty?'

Maulānā Rūmi, in the fifth book of the *Maṣnavi*, tells a tale of 'the lover who recounted before the beloved his loyal services, laid bare his helplessness and finally asked if there were any other service he could perform'. On this the beloved replied: 'All this you have done but you have left undone the one thing necessary: dying to self, abandonment of self. You have tackled the branches, not the root. You are still alive, still living in yourself. Come, now, die if you are a lover who lays down his life. Die, and you will find life in its fulness.'

In his *Teẕkeret al Awliyā* Sheikh 'Aṭṭār illustrates one of the effects of absorption in God by an incident in the life of Bāyazid Bisṭāmi. Bāyazid had a disciple who had been with him for twenty years but whose name he could never remember. The young man one day told him he was genuinely grieved that, after twenty years, his master could still not remember his name. The sheikh replied: 'I am not mocking you. *His* name has come to me and has shut out all other names from my mind. I learn your name and soon forget it again!'

If there is one point on which all Ṣūfis are agreed, it is this need to get rid of self in order to reach God. That old vintage mystic Abū Saïd said: 'Wherever some thought of yourself is, there is hell. Wherever you are not, there is heaven.' And he added, on another occasion: The veil between the servant and his Lord is neither heaven nor earth, neither throne nor threshold. The real veil is your egotism, your thinking of yourself. Get rid of that and you reach God.

Another occasional effect of mystical absorption is insensibility. Abul Khair Aqta' had a diseased hand. The doctors decided the hand would have to be amputated. As he would not consent to this, his disciples advised them to wait until the Sheikh entered into prayer, when he became quite insensible. They followed this advice and it was only when he came out of prayer that he found that his hand had been amputated.

In the case of a number of great mystics, this state of trance or insensibility was interrupted when it was time to recite the namāz or ritual prayer. As soon as this was finished, the mystic returned at once, involuntarily, into the state of trance. This is recorded of Shibli and of Nūri, to mention but two. The phenomenon is known as *jam' wa tafriqa* (union and separation).

Mystical knowledge of God may also have as a by-product the quality known as *firāsat,* or supernatural perspicacity extending to facts relating to created affairs. A number of stories are told of this sort of second sight through which Ṣūfis, celebrated for their mystical absorption, were aware of what was happening to people at a great distance.

More drastic, however, were the claims made by some Ṣūfis on the basis of the inner light which illumined their hearts. Often, this 'inner light' moved them to conduct at variance with received notions as to orthodoxy or propriety. Stricter theologians found dangers in this recourse to an inner, personal criterion.

On the fringes of this zone of inner light, in bright clusters or in dark writhing shapes, are the *khaṭarāt wa vasāvis* (good thoughts or bad). Ṣūfis inclined to be *ahl i khāṭir*—devotees of the first thought that enters the mind, as this is considered to come direct from God and not as the result of reflection.

It is related of Khair an-Nassáj that one day a thought came to him that Junayd was at the door. He repelled the thought as a distraction. The same thought recurred, only to be repelled again. At last he went to the door and opened it. There stood Junayd.

EIGHT

THE VISION OF GOD

IN Christian theology vision of God is a reward, a consummation, reserved for the next life. In this life 'no man has seen God at any time'. The Ṣūfis, on the contrary, reject this *fardāyi zāhiḍ* (devotee's tomorrow), to use the expression of Ḥāfiz. They are intent on the here and now. The word *mushāhada* itself contains the notion of direct vision, *shuhūd*. The soul, by the fact of its spiritual and intellectual nature, is invited by God to behold Him and He will grant this favour to all who serve Him sincerely and whole-heartedly. The necessary condition for the divine revelation is not so much physical death as a mystical death, death to self. Self is a veil, a hindrance to sight of Him. It must disappear if God is to appear. God is, indeed, all that really exists. The rest is only appearance. Appearance glows and fades on the unchanging background of Being. Still, in the nature of things, God is free to reveal Himself or to conceal Himself. If He reveals Himself to His servant, that will be a free gift of His grace. It follows, then, that the preliminary disposition of *fanā* (disappearance of self) is also an effect of grace, it cannot be achieved by a man's own efforts. Still, it could never be achieved at all did not man's spiritual nature, witnessed to by the Qorānic *nafakhnā fihi min rūḥinā* (we breathed into him of our Spirit), possess already the root of the matter, setting no limit to the scope of his knowledge and spiritual experience. It is true that a great mystic like 'Aṭṭār can say:

'The mind does not reach to the frontier of Thy perfection.
'The soul does not reach of itself the Palace of Union (*viṣāl*).
'Were all the atoms of the world to become eyes,

'They could never comprehend Thy infinite Beauty.
And
'This reason of mine, which for long I made my guide,
'I have consumed in the effort to know God.
'My whole life has been spent and with this weak reason I have learnt
'This much alone: that I still know Him not.'

But 'Aṭṭār is here speaking only of the unaided human reason (*'aql*) and, moreover, he is thinking of the infinite nature of the divine object, which will always, necessarily, transcend the powers of a finite mind. Lahiji compares the discursive reason to the stick of a blind man. He needs, nevertheless, to be guided by one who sees, and this kind of sight is peculiar to prophets, saints and mystics, granted only in reward for an obedience and devotion involving body, mind, heart and spirit. The vision of God is granted to a heart in love with Him and constantly seeking Him. 'Aṭṭār has also the following quatrain:

'The heart is in love with Thy face with a sincere faith,
'The soul has been seeking union with Thee from the very first.
'One who did not seek union with Thee found nothing.
'He who found Thee, seeks nothing else.'

As another writer puts it: *Nāgāh miyāyad vali bar dil i āgāh miyāyad* (He comes unheralded, but He comes to none but an awakened heart).

Men are divided up into various great groups in accordance with the use they make of their faculties. Apart from those who let their sensual faculties predominate, there are many who choose a life in which the reasoning and discursive faculties take the lion's share and who are content to restrict their field of action to the things of sense and to win their successes there. Quite a number of these, indeed, refuse to admit the existence of any objects or values beyond this material field, open to exact measurement, and shut their minds, on principle, against any divine illumination or extracorporeal experience. The remaining category consists of those who subordinate temporal things to the search for spiritual and eternal things. These are the *ahl i dil* (men of heart), God's sincere and trusted friends. It is upon these that He pours out gifts of the spirit, including mystical knowledge, resignation and unbounded trust in God.

Men of this kind are not long content to worship God blindly and undiscerningly. Their love of God urges them to seek an increasingly intimate and delicate knowledge of Him. Thus of 'Ali (to whom Persian mystics trace back the living chain—(*silsileh*)—of spiritual tradition) it was asked: 'Do you see God?' and he replied: 'I do not worship a God whom I do not see.'

This intimate, infused knowledge of God, then, is not arrived at by any process of discursive thought, by the elucidation of rational proofs. God's beauty is rendered visible to hearts that love Him by the diffusion in them of His own essential light. In a well-known line of his *Maṣnavi*, Rūmi says that the sun is its own evidence: *Aftāb āmad dalil i āftāb*. And so Nūri, asked what is the proof of God, replied: 'God'. He added that 'whenever the Lord conceals Himself from someone, such a one is entirely deprived of proof or knowledge of Him'. (*Jāmi, Nafahāt ul Uns.*) If God (in the *Sūrat an Nūr*[1]) is compared to the light in a lamp set in a niche, the niche, we must know, is the believing and loving heart. From this source springs, not dry-as-dust knowledge (*'ilm,* science) but that intimate knowledge gained in contact with a kindred spirit, a living personality. Hence it is called *'ilm ladunni*—knowledge derived from the divine Presence Itself. This is *Ḥāl* (mystical experience), not *qāl* (hearsay), not 'what my dad told me' but 'what my Lord showed me'.

One who has thus soared beyond the dust and reached the realm of undimmed sunlight can no longer be said to walk by faith. So Rūmi, in the first book of the *Maṣnavi*, declares:

> 'One whose *miḥrāb* (the prayer corner turned towards Mecca) has become the divine essence itself

[1] Sura 24 of *Qorān*.

'Would be wrong to go plodding on in the way of faith.
'One who has become the King's Privy Chamberlain
'Could only lose by engaging in trade on the King's behalf.'

In his *Divān i Shams Tabriz* the same poet asks:

'When the sun shines out, where is the dusk of doubt, or, for the matter of that, where is the lamp of belief? Faith says: Come on, and doubt says: Go back. But when the soul with undimmed radiance lights up the body, "forward" and "backward" no longer make sense.'

To have been granted the favour of this vision of God in the heart is an incomparable blessing. Sari Saqati is quoted in the *Kashf ul Mahjūb* (Zhukovski's edition, p. 137) as follows:

'O my God, send me any torment or affliction you will, except that of being deprived of the contemplation of Thy face, for when I behold Thy beauty I am able to bear any suffering, whereas, when I am deprived of it, even Thy kindnesses and mercies are hard for me to bear. The most painful torment of hell is to be shut out from the sight of Thee. In Paradise no bliss is to be compared with the revelation of Thy Face. To be veiled from Thee is no better than ruin and damnation. So (Sari continues) God's way is to give His servant's heart the grace of beholding Him, whatever the vicissitudes through which his soul is passing, in order that he may be able to endure all torments and trials and penitential practices by reason of the sweetness of that delicious taste (*shirb*).'

It was told of Bāyazid Bisṭāmi that, when asked how old he was, he replied: 'Four years.' 'How is that?' 'For seventy years I lived under the veil of this world. For only four years I have been seeing Him. Those veiled years I do not count as part of my life.'

Bāyazid also said: 'So long as one knows it is God (that one is seeing), the revelation is not entire. When it is entire, one can no longer reflect on it consciously.'

This state may arise, says Hujviri[1] either from the fulness of certainty (*yaqin*) or from the conquering power of love. Thus when Muḥammad ibn Wāsi' said: 'I never saw anything without seeing God in it', it was from fulness of faith and certainty. When Shibli said: 'I saw nothing at all but God', he was carried away by the impetuosity of love, by the divine *jazba* or attraction.

[1] Op. cit., p. 47.

NINE

TWO ṢŪFI PRACTICES

HAVING now studied, all too briefly, the chief motives of the Ṣūfi quest and the chief heads of their doctrine, before bidding them farewell, it would complete our knowledge of them to view them engaged upon two of their favourite practices, one, distinctly serious, the *ẕikr,* the other, apparently more frivolous, *samá'*.

I. ZIKR

It is not easy to find a single English term for the word *zikr*. In itself it means 'remembrance'. As used by the mystics, it denotes the devout invocation and repetition of the holy Name of God, either alone or enshrined in some formula.

The *zikr* par excellence is the *shahádeh,* or, at any rate, that part of which relates to God alone. 'There is no god but God'—*Lā ilāha illā 'llāh.* This formula is often recited by the devout while they sway gently from side to side.

A number of religious confraternities (*ṭariqas*) have their own form of *zikr,* constituting the service performed by the brethren, grouped together, often on a Thursday evening (eve of the sacred day of Friday, *shab i jum'a*). A *ẕikr* may, however, and often is, gone through in private by single individuals.

The words should be repeated a great many times, with as great a degree of intense concentration as can be summoned up. Attention should be centred more and more on the meaning or spiritual reality of what is said, until the *zákir* (remembrancer) is not so much busied with the *ẕikr* (remembrance) as with the *mazkúr* (the one invoked or remembered).

If the Ṣūfi masters attached so much importance to the practice of *ẓikr*, in the sense explained, it was because they held it to be the best way to impress the mind and to set up the conditions for the achievement of close attention and the concentration of the soul's powers on that which is the very purpose of the mystical journey. This combination of meditation and invocation produces a climate of confidence and certainty in the soul and prepares it for the state of contemplation, which is the wayfarer's goal and object. Ghazáli, in his Persian work, the *Kimiyāyi Sa'ādat* ('Philosopher's stone of Happiness'), as well as in his great work in Arabic, the *Iḥyā 'Ulūm ed Din*, enters into great detail as to the nature and the advantages of this practice. The first degree in it, 'Common Invocation', even though it may amount simply to the external invocation of the holy name, is of value, 'since it denotes that the state of carelessness and indifference has been set aside'. Indeed, one who has dismissed carelessness (*ghiflat*) is already a *ẓākir*, even if his tongue be silent.

A higher degree comes when the *ẓākir* 'tears off the veil of reason and with his whole heart fixes his attention on the Lord'. The highest degree of all is that of the *ẓākir* who becomes *fāni* (lost) in truth—that is God. At first the adept has constantly to take pains lest his soul drift back into its natural state of carelessness and inattention. But as he acquires greater mastery, the *ẓikr* takes such a hold on him that it can with difficulty be driven out by any other thought or fancy. The supreme degree, however, comes when the one invoked takes possession of the heart, for, as Ghazáli says, there is a great difference between one who loves the invoked one and one who loves the invocation. Perfection lies in this, that the invocation and all consciousness of it vanish from the heart and He who is invoked alone remains there.

This, however, is not in the power of the disciple, however earnestly he strives. It is a pure gift of grace to which he can do no more than offer himself. That is no excuse for failing to do one's part, for, as Rūmi says in the sixth Book of the *Maṣnavi*,

'The root of the matter is a divine attraction and yet, dear fellow,
'Do what you can and do not put a stop to that attraction.'

In another passage of the *Maṣnavi*, book three, vv. 180 and onwards, Rūmi relates that God most high told Moses: Call upon me with a mouth with which thou has not sinned. Moses replied that he had not such a mouth. 'Call unto me then by the mouth of others . . . Act in such wise that their mouths may pray for thee in the nights and days.' The poet goes on: 'Praise of God is pure: when purity comes, defilement packs up and goes out. When the holy name (the Persian word *pāk* signifies both pure and holy) comes into the mouth, neither impurity remains nor any sorrow.'

In the subsequent passage, Rūmi, as is his wont, lifts the whole subject of the *ẕikr* onto a higher plane. It is headed, 'Showing that the supplicant's invocation of God is essentially the same thing as God's reponse to him'.

'One night a certain man was crying "Allāh" till his lips were growing sweet with praise of Him.

'The Devil said, "Prithee, O garrulous one, where is the response 'Here am I' to all this 'Allāh'?"

'Broken-hearted, the man laid down his head to sleep. In a dream he saw Khaḍir (legendary figure of a saint who stood also for the perfect spiritual director) amid the verdure.

'Khaḍir said to him, "Hark, you have ceased praising God: how is it that you repent of having called upon Him?"

'He replied, "No 'Here am I' (*Ar.* '*labbaika*, the customary response of the faithful when they hear the Muezzin's call to prayer) comes to me in response, so I fear lest I be a reprobate, turned away from His door."

'Said Khaḍir, "(God saith), That 'Allāh' of thine *is* my 'Here am I', and that supplication and grief and ardour of thine is my messenger to thee. . . . Beneath every 'O Lord' of thine is many a 'Here am I' (from me)".'

The name of some saint or of some beloved person may be so intimately and inseparably linked with that of God in the mind and heart of an invoker that it may take the place of the holy name itself. Thus we are told that Sheikh Abū'l Qāsim Gurgāni invoked God under the name of the revered saint Oveis. Maulānā Rūmi tells how Zuleikha called everything 'Joseph', in order thus to enjoy hearing often the beloved name. The poet goes on: 'The common people call constantly on the holy name; when holy love is wanting, such action has little effect. When the soul is united with Truth, to invoke one is to invoke the other. If Jesus spoke of God as he did, that was because being empty of self, he was full of love for the Friend. A jug can pour forth only what it contains.'

One of the most valuable treasure-houses of Persian spiritual and mystical wisdom is the *Mirṣād ul 'Ibād* (The Broad Way of the Servants of God) of Sheikh Najmeddin Rāzi, known as Dāya. This work was completed at Sivās in Anatolia, whither the sheikh had fled from the advancing and devastating Mongol invasion in 1223. His own spiritual Director, Najmeddin Kubrā, had perished in the storming of Khwarazm (the modern Khiva) by Jenghiz Khan in 1221. Jenghiz had heard of this remarkable saint and thaumaturgus and offered him his life, but the sheikh refused to ingratiate himself with the bloodstained tyrant and perished with hundreds of thousands of other victims. Najmeddin Dāya himself died in a.h. 654 (A.D. 1256).

It is devoutly to be wished that some scholar would edit and translate the *Mirṣād*: it would be worth a dozen Western works on Persian mysticism, however well-informed and well-intentioned.

The third part of the work is concerned with the various elements contributing to the spiritual development of man, in his psycho-physical nature: the Prophets (in the broad, Islamic sense of the word), the Law, the spiritual discipline of the mystical Way (*Ṭariqat*), including the function of the sheikh or spiritual guide, the place of *ẓikr*, the need of solitude, the part played in man's perfection by supernatural revelations, visions and so forth, and, finally, his attaining to union with God 'without identification and without separation'.

It is worth while studying in some detail what Dāya has to teach the Moslem disciple of the Path regarding the performance of the *ẓikr*, in the sense we have already seen.

As is his wont, he begins by reference to the fundamental Qorānic texts relating to the matter, such as 'Remember me and I will remember you' (*Surat al Baqara*) and 'Call God often to mind, that it may be well with you' (*Surat al Jum'a*). Then he quotes the *ḥadith* (traditional saying) of the Prophet Mahomet: 'The noblest *ẓikr* is *Lā ilāha illā' llāh* (There is no god but God).'

He then points out that *ẓikr* or remembrance centred on the repetition of some devout formula, is opposed to *nisyān*, forgetfulness. In the *Surat al Kahf*[1] we read: 'Remember me when you have forgotten'—meaning, as Dāya declares, 'when you have forgotten all else but Me', since only thus will a man's *ẓikr* be pure. When, in remembering God, a man also remembers himself, the act is tainted with virtual idolatry or duality. When our mind is filled with the remembrance of created things, it falls short of the pure remembrance of God alone and, in the last resort, forgets God altogether, whereupon Almighty God forgets us, lets us escape from the remembrance of His mercy. 'They forgot God and He forgot them' (*Surat at-Tawba*).[2] This spiritual disease is cured by its contrary. Hence, from the dispensary of the *Qorān* He gave them this medicine: 'Remember God often', so that by much remembrance they might be delivered from the films and incrustations of great forgetfulness and from the affliction of that malady. ('That you may prosper.')

Such benefits accrue particularly from the use of *Lā ilāha illā' llāh* which is 'the good utterance which rises to Him' (*Surat al Fāṭir*).[3] On the positive side its medicinal property is attributed to the Prophet's recommendation. On the side of its essence and meaning, the value comes from its contents: both negation (*lā ilāha*, there is no god) and affirmation (*illāllāh*,—save God alone). Thus, by inculcating the remem-

[1] Sura 18 of *Qorán*.
[2] Sura 9 of *Qorán*.
[3] Sura 35, v. 10.

brance of God alone, the *ẓikr* is stripped of the clothing of letters and forms and in the glory of the light of the sublime deity, the property of *Kullu shayin hālikun illā wajhahu* (All passes away except His face) is made manifest.

The human spirit and its very remembrance is swallowed up in the ocean of 'Remember me' and by the power and grace of 'I will remember you', *ẓikr*, *ẓakir* and *maẓkūr* (the remembrance, the one who remembers and the One remembered) are merged in one, banishing all polytheism. Joseph Hussein Rāzi's remark is here borne out, that 'None said God but God'. Dāya then quotes a couplet:

> 'Hamstring the whole of creation with the knife of *lā ilāha*,
> 'In order that the whole world may make room for the Prince of *Illā' llāh*.'

The sheikh then turns to what he calls the 'nature, proper conditions and good manners' of the *ẓikr*. In expounding this part of His theme he bases himself on two Qoranic texts: 'The Lord said: Remember God as you do your own parents, or even more vividly' (*Surat al Baqara*) and again: 'Remember your Lord in yourself with compunction and awe' (*Surat Al 'Imrān*).

Hence a fervent disciple must found his practice of *ẓikr* on a sincere repentance for all his sins, betokened, if possible, by a ritual bath or at least the complete ablutions (*wuẓu'*) . . . Let him put on clean clothes, true cleanliness consisting of freedom from dirt, from injustice, from any prohibition (e.g. clothes of silk) and from extravagance—i.e. they should be not flowing but brief.

Having prepared a room which is empty, dark and clean, in which he will, for preference, burn some sweet-scented incense, let him sit there, cross-legged, facing the *qibla* (direction of Mekka). Laying his hands on his thighs, let him stir up his heart to wakefulness, keeping a guard on his eyes. Then with profound veneration he should say aloud *Lā ilāha illā' llāh*. The *lā ilāha* should be fetched from the root of the navel and the *illā' llāh* drawn into the heart, so that the powerful effects of the *ẕikr* may make themselves felt in all the limbs and organs. But let him not raise his voice too loud. He should strive, as far as possible, to damp and lower it, according to the words 'Invoke thy Lord in thyself humbly and with compunction, without publicity of speech' (*Surat al A'raf*).

After this fashion, then, he will utter the *ẕikr* frequently and intently, thinking in his heart on the meaning of it and banishing every distraction. When he thinks of *lā ilāha*, he should tell himself: I want nothing, seek nothing, love nothing *illā' llāh*—but God. Thus, with *lā ilāha* he denies and excludes all competing objects and with *illā' llāh* he affirms and posits the divine Majesty as the sole object loved, sought and aimed at.

In each *ẕikr* his heart should be aware and present (*ḥāzir*) from start to finish, with denial and affirmation. If he finds in his heart something to which he is attached, let him not regard it but give his attention to the divine Majesty, seeking the grace of help from the holy patronage of his spiritual Father. With the negation *lā ilāha* let him wipe out that attachment, uprooting the love of that thing from his heart, and with *illā' llāh* let him set up in its place the love of Truth (God). By perseverance and assiduity in this practice he will slowly but surely wean his heart from all (created) loves and affections.

You should know, says Dāya, that the heart (or soul) is the secret presence-chamber of God, since (*ḥadith*): 'My earth cannot contain me nor my heaven. Only the heart of my believing servant can contain me', and as long as the throng of Others is found in the Audience Chamber of the heart, His Majesty will not appear. Only when the Sergeant at Arms of *lā ilāha* clears the Presence Chamber of this throng of others can we expect the glory of King *Illāllāh* to draw nigh.

'Clean the place out, the King will come unawares.
'Only when it is empty does the King enter His pavilion.'

Dāya then explains the importance of learning the *ẕikr*

from the teaching and example of a perfect spiritual teacher. He begins by distinguishing between two kinds of *ẓikr*: *taqlidi* and *taḥqiqi*—that is, one that is simply repetition and one that is charged with original investigation or exploration. It is, of course, this second type of *ẓikr* that the Master desires. It falls into the prepared soil of a disciple's heart through the action and inspiration of a holy teacher, a fruit of his holy intimacy (*uns*) with God, just as the master himself received the sacred deposit from another saint and fostered it in his heart under the rain and sunshine of his Father's blessing, so that it grew in its turn into a tree of holiness, bringing forth the fruits of invocation from the blossoms of 'I will remember you'. Then, in the perfect ripeness of the rank of master (sheikh), he sowed a seed in the soil of the disciple's heart. Constantly cultivated, it grows day by day, till great branches shoot forth and the tree of mystical knowledge is reared.

Before the inauguration of his training, the disciple should fast for three days, during which time he should strive to be always purified by ablution and constantly occupied in devout ejaculations, even when moving about. He should mix little with men and speak only as much as is strictly necessary. He should be very sparing at table and watch longer hours in prayer and silent intercession by night. After those three days, under the Sheikh's directions, let him take a ritual bath, forming the intention of undergoing the baptism of Islām, just as happened to each one in the beginning, when he first sought religion: I mean that first of all he received the baptism of Islám and then learnt the lesson of the word (*La ilāha*, etc.) from the master so now he should take the baptism of Islām in its spiritual reality. As the water is poured over him, let him say: Oh Lord, I have taken this outward cleansing with water. With the regard of Thy grace and mercy do Thou purify my heart which is the scene of Thy operation.

When the bath is finished, after night prayers, he should present himself to the sheikh who will set him facing the *qibla* while he himself remains with his back to the *qibla*. He will sit kneeling at the sheikh's service, hands folded, heart alert. The sheikh gives him some appropriate exhortation and says a few words as to the secrets of the *ẓikr* and the method of inculcating it, so that the disciple may become sufficiently recollected. The latter, withdrawing his heart from all else, keeps it facing the sheikh's heart, in a gesture of deep yearning and unbounded expectation. Then the sheikh says once, in a loud, strong voice, *Lā ilāha illā' llāh.* The novice then says, *Lā ilāha,* etc. in the same tone and voice as the sheikh. Then twice more in the same way. Finally the sheikh pronounces a blessing to which the novice answers Amen. He then goes back to his hermitage and sitting there cross-legged, facing the *qibla,* he starts fostering the seed of *ẓikr.*

The word (*Lā ilāha,* etc.) is 'like a good tree, whose roots are firm and whose branches reach out to heaven' (*Qorān, Surat Ibrahim*). The learner should therefore strive to bring it about that the roots of this mystical tree should reach all his limbs and every particle of his being. When the *ẓikr* has been thus firmly rooted in the soil of the soul, it begins to draw the heart upwards towards heaven. In this phase, the heart (i.e. soul) takes up the *ẓikr* from the tongue. When the heart begins to recite, the tongue should stop. When the heart stops, the tongue must go to it. Thus the *ẓikr* develops and pushes upwards to the heights until it reaches its perfection and its end, which is in the presence of the divine Majesty, for 'unto Him rises the good word' (Sura of the Angels).

When the tree reaches the fullness of perfection, the blossoms of contemplation appear on the tips of the branches and from these gradually emerge the fruits of revelations and supernatural visions. One of these fruits is the station of unity (*tawḥid*). This is a great secret, containing the purpose of creation and the sum of the secrets of the world invisible.

I have translated these sections of the *Mirṣād* in full, omitting only a few needless *longueurs* and repetitions, in order that the reader may have before him an example of a Ṣūfi instruction, unaltered and without modification of any kind. In them we can see the devout Moslem, faithful to scriptural tradition—which, indeed he interprets at times with the latitude of a Ṣūfi mystic concerned as much with the seventy-seven inner meanings as with the literal sense—and to the traditional practice of the *Ṭariqa*, with its somewhat naïf realism, while ready, at any moment, to let himself be carried off by the gales of lyrical fervour. In Dāya we have a good example of the prudent and responsible middle way, which, on the whole, constitutes the solid framework of the Ṣūfi mystical system.

2. SAMĀʿ (AUDITION)

The other method much favoured by the Ṣūfis, in the wake of the great ecstatic Jalāl ed Din Rūmi, with a view to encouraging and reinforcing ecstasy and trance, is known as *samáʿ*, literally 'listening' or audition.

It must be remembered that all Persian poetry, the mystical sort not least, is intended to be chanted, either to a regular tune or in free musical improvisation. Each type of poem has its own appropriate chant. The best performers combine a formal chant with occasional outbursts of improvisation. The best known chant of this kind, as might have been expected, is that to which the *Maṣnavi* of Maulānā Rūmi is sung. The Persians are very sensitive to the influence of music and song. The strict Arabic Moslems of the primitive school are, on the contrary, rather puritanical in this respect and frown upon music, song and dance, which are never inculcated in the *Qorān*. When the Ṣūfis began to introduce mystical concerts and dances into their régime they were roundly reproached and condemned by the old orthodox school. This did not stop them. Rūmi and his followers gave themselves up without compunction to the ecstasy caused by the *samāʿ* (audition) of instrumental music or of songs which, on the face of it, often expressed profane love. Dancing was also pressed into the service of the mystical spirit. Rūmi composed some of his most wonderful lyrics and couplets while gyrating endlessly round a column in his convent (*khānegāh*).

Indeed the principal *ẕikr* of the Order of Mevlevi dervishes which he founded may be said to have consisted in the planetary round where the brethren, in a white-robed circle, recited the *ẕikr* in a form which became more and more simplified, as they swayed up and down, awaiting the entrance of the chief performer who spun round, arms extended, in their midst for an incredibly long time. This figure is thought to have represented the solar system and recalled, perhaps, the deep-rooted mystical belief in the music of the spheres, of which earthly music and rhythm are ecstasy-causing reminders (*anamnesis*).

To the Christian—or perhaps, rather to the Westerner—such practices may well appear extravagant and dangerous. The Ṣūfis themselves were not unaware of this possible danger and pointed out that the *samā*ʿ bore good fruit only with those who approached it in the right dispositions. But it may well be that the use of music and song in the Christian liturgy itself was originally intended to induce a sort of religious enthusiasm or ecstasy. Rightly listened to, the liturgical chant would set up a tendency to trance. We can see something similar in the life of St Theresa—the fact that she was a Spaniard may not be altogether unconnected with it. Frequently she passed into ecstasy when one of her daughters sang in recreation an impassioned mystical love-song to Jesus.

The Ṣūfis held that the continuous, steady rhythms of music had the effect of disposing the soul for contemplation, whereas violent and discordant noises have the opposite effect. In his monograph on music, Avicenna declares that 'all the old tunes of Khorasan and Persia are in continuous rhythms, which help to regularise and pacify the soul'. Music, in fact, like any other manifestation of beauty, has the effect of leading the soul up to, and plunging it in the source of beauty. Conversely, one who is habitually drawn to God (*majẕūb*) hears His lauds and praises in every lovely melody. The true mystic, however, passes rapidly through the 'heard melodies' to 'those unheard'. Outward forms fade from his consciousness and his soul becomes absorbed in the inner meaning and reality of that which is hinted at by outward signs. To be glued to the outward forms would be unworthy of him and, indeed, the consummate mystic has no further use for such crutches. Still, the unity of the human system is such that every spiritual state, however profoundly seated, tends to translate itself in bodily forms of expression, in song or dance. The awkward dichotomy of the self-conscious Westener is unknown to the complete, emancipated Ṣūfi. Similar outbursts of mystical exultation and jubilation have been recorded in the lives of a number of Christian Saints. There is no need to suppose that all high mystical states immobilize the body. Did not the Psalmist sing: 'My heart and my flesh have exulted in the living God'? It could not be otherwise for those who have the 'hearing ear', for those who, in the words of Mullah Hādi Sabzevāri, 'have, like Moses, an ear that discerns mysteries'. These are moved to ecstatic yearning and desire, not merely by the chant of the *Qorān* or the call of the Muezzin, but by the song of a peasant wafted across the fields, by the wailing of the violin or the song of birds: all can be, are destined to be, *hātifu'l ghaib*, a messenger from the invisible world.

On this account—because music is a 'burnisher of the soul' and brings it into a state of equilibrium, clarity, tenderness and delicacy, thus contributing to its perfection, all the Ṣūfis, with the exception of a few jejune and narrow-minded sects, like the Naqshbandis, followers of Bahā edDin Naqshband of Bukhārā, give themselves up without compunction to these sacred concerts.

Maulānā Rūmi, in the fourth book of the *Maṣnavi*, singing of Ibrahim son of Adham, who abandoned his kingdom of Khorāsān in order to devote himself to heavenly experience, says (in Professor Nicholson's translation):

> 'His object in listening to the sound of the rebeck was, like that of ardent lovers of God, to bring to his mind the phantasy of that divine allocution. . . . Hence philosophers have said that we received these harmonies from the revolution of the celestial sphere. But true believers

say that the influences of Paradise made every unpleasant sound to be beautiful.

'We have all been parts of Adam, we have heard those melodies in Paradise.

'Although the water and earth of our bodies have caused a doubt to fall upon us, something of those melodies comes back to our memory.

'Therefore *samā'* (music) is the food of lovers (of God), since therein is the phantasy of composure: the fire of love is kindled by melodies.'

In the same strain, Sheikh Sa'ad edDin Hamavi, one of the companions of Najmeddin Kubrā, and himself a notable mystic of the seventh century of the hijra, wrote these lines:

'When music is heard, the soul scents the perfume of the Beloved; melody, like a mystic barque, transports it to the shores of the Friend.'

The following story, related in the life of Abū Saïd of Mihna, composed by Muhammad b. Munavvar, throws an amusing light upon the diversity of views prevailing here and there in the Muslim world as to the lawfulness or otherwise of music and song. It relates that, when the sheikh was at Qain, a notable Imām of that place, the Imām Muhammad Qaini, came to greet him and thenceforward became his constant companion and admirer, going with him even to exercises of mystical song. On one of these occasions our sheikh passed into a state of ecstasy which communicated itself to the entire company. The time was passing pleasantly thus when the Muezzin's call for the midday prayer made itself heard. The sheikh and his followers continued their ecstatic dance, interspersed with shouts and groans. In the midst of all this, the Imām Muhammad called out: 'Prayers, prayers!' To this the sheikh replied: 'We *are* at prayer!' and went on dancing. The Imām left them and went off to perform his ritual devotions like a good Moslem.

A further reason for the Ṣūfis' devotion to music and song lay in this, that their outlook on life was fundamentally one of open-hearted joy and exultation, so impetuous as to surge over the dark barrier of death. Sheikh Ṣalāh-eddin Zarkūb, the successor of Jalālu' ddin Rūmi as head of the Mevlevi Order, laid it down in his will that there should be no mourning at his funeral, but that, since he had been delivered from this world's house of grief, and had been admitted to the joy of eternal life, he should be committed to the earth with music and song, 'so that' (as Sulṭān Walad, Rūmi's son, put it in a poem):

'So that men may know that God's chosen ones
'Go out to the meeting with joy and laughter.
'Their death is a festival of rejoicing,
'Their dwelling is amid the houris in Paradise.'

And so it was done.

A sound, middle-of-the-way view of the effects of 'audition' is expressed by the poet Saadi in the following verses:

'I will not say, my brother, what *samā*' is
'Before I know who the listener is.
'If the bird has flown from the dove-cote of meaning,
'Even an angel will fall short of its achievement.
'If the listener is a frivolous and flippant man,
'The devil in his brain is but strengthened by it.
'Flowers are scattered by the morning breeze,
'Wood no: the axe alone can split that.'

In another passage the same poet justifies the Ṣūfi dance in the following way:

'Do not blame the bewildered dervish:
'If he waves his hands and feet, the reason is that he is drowning . . .
'The dance opens a door in the soul to divine influences,
'It spreads wide the hands to all things created.
'The dance is good when it arises from remembrance of the Beloved.
'Then each waving sleeve has a soul in it.
'If you set out bravely to swim,

'You can best shake arms and legs when divested of clothing;
'Strip off the robes of earthly honour and of hypocrisy:
'A drowning man is hampered by his clothes.'

References to 'doffing' or 'tearing up' one's robe or dervish's habit (*muraqqa*ʿ or *khirqa*)—as in the last two verses of Saadi's poem, just quoted—are frequent in Ṣūfi literature and describe the custom of many dervishes, who, when beside themselves with mystical effervescence, threw their habit, or scraps of it, to the singers or to others who might be present, these shreds and tatters being then looked upon as precious relics. Such practices, at least in a metaphorical sense, were, of course, dear to the heart of Ḥāfiẓ of Shirāz.

The importance attached by many Ṣūfis to music and the dance has some relation to their cult of beauty. Since all earthly beauty is a revelation and a symbol of the heavenly beauty which is its cause and exemplar, to pay due court to it must help men to pass over to spiritual and absolute beauty and perfection: 'The allegorical is the bridge to the reality.' Leaders along this way were men like Aḥmad Ghazzāli, brother of the famous theologian, Fakhreddin ʿIrāqi and Awḥadeddin Kermāni. For them the love of beauty is the chief guide on the way of perfection. They held that our nature makes it impossible for us to reach the formless beauty save through created forms, which, in accordance with their habit of defying Pharisees and Philistines, they often refer to as 'idols' (*butān*). The homage paid to an 'idol' is, in reality, directed to the One it represents and symbolizes. Kermāni:

'If my bodily eye gazes on created forms of beauty,
'That is because outward forms bear the impress of the inner meaning.
'We live in a world of forms and images
'And we cannot behold realities otherwise than through images and forms.'

This view was at the origin of the specialized meaning of the word *shāhid*. It has come to mean 'beloved' or 'charmer' because a lovely being was considered to be a 'witness' of the divine beauty.

Unregenerate nature, however, needs a great deal of ascetic and moral training before the mind can safely find its way through physical beauty to the divine. This entrancing vision, as the Beatitudes remind us, is reserved for the pure in heart.

INDEX